New Selected Poems 1966–1987

by Seamus Heaney

Luke McBratney

Series Editors:
Nicola Onyett and Luke McBratney

HODDER EDUCATION
AN HACHETTE UK COMPANY

The publisher would like to thank the following for permission to reproduce copyright material:

Acknowledgments:

Throughout: Seamus Heaney: from *New Selected Poems: 1966–1987* (Faber & Faber, 1990), by permission of Faber & Faber Ltd.; **pp.ix, 1, 2, 9, 11, 27: Seamus Heaney:** from *Preoccupations: Selected Prose 1968–1978* (Faber & Faber, 1984), by permission of Faber & Faber Ltd.; **pp.3, 4, 12, 13, 16, 18, 22, 31, 34, 35, 43, 58, 59, 65, 66, 70: Dennis O'Driscoll:** from *Stepping Stones Interviews with Seamus Heaney* (Faber & Faber, 2008), by permission of Faber & Faber Ltd.; **pp.7, 8, 15, 19, 22, 32: Michael Parker:** from *The Making of the Poet* (Gill and Macmillan, 1993) reprinted with permission of Michael Parker; **p.10: Patricia Craig:** from 'TP Flanagan: Artist and teacher whose work inspired Seamus Heaney', *The Independent* (18 April 2011), http://www.independent.co.uk/news/obituaries/tp-flanagan-artist-and-teacher-whose-work-inspired-seamus-heaney-2269579.html © The Independent 2016, reprinted with permission; **pp.19, 28, 71, 75: Helen Vendler:** from *Seamus Heaney* (Harvard University Press, 2000), reprinted with permission; **pp.19, 29, 72: E. Andrews:** from *The Poetry of Seamus Heaney* (Columbia University Press, 1998), reprinted with permission; **pp.22, 49, 54: Bernard O'Donoghue:** from *The Cambridge Companion to Seamus Heaney* (Cambridge University Press, 2009), reprinted with permission; **pp.23, 46, 56, 58, 63, 66: Neil Corcoran:** from *The Poetry of Seamus Heaney: A critical study* (Faber & Faber, 1998), by permission of Faber & Faber Ltd.; **p.38: Seamus Heaney:** in *Ploughshares,* ed. James Randall (Issue 18, 1979), reprinted with permission; **p.40: Seamus Heaney:** quoted in John Haffenden *Seamus Heaney Viewpoints: Poets in Conversation* (Faber & Faber, 1981); **pp.61–2: George Morgan:** from 'An Interview with Seamus Heaney', *Cycnos* (Vol. 15 No. 2, July 2008), http://revel.unice.fr/cycnos/?id=1594.

Every effort has been made to trace or contact all copyright holders, but if any have been inadvertently overlooked the Publishers will be pleased to make the necessary arrangements at the first opportunity.

Photo credits:

p.10 © Boglands (for Seamus Heaney), 1967, acrylic and pastel on board, 91.5 x 122 cm. © Estate of T.P. Flanagan.; **p.25** © Hemis / Alamy Stock Photo; **p.33** © TopFoto; **p.46** © Shutterstock / Everett - Art; **p.53** © Fox Photos/Getty Images; **p.62** © ihervas - Fotolia; **p.72** © Frederick Hoare/Central Press/Getty Images; **p.76** © Wellcome Library, London/Creative Commons Attribution only licence CC BY 4.0 http://creativecommons.org/licenses/by/4.0/; **p.80** © David Levenson/Getty Images; **p.83** © TopFoto

Although every effort has been made to ensure that website addresses are correct at time of going to press, Hodder Education cannot be held responsible for the content of any website mentioned. It is sometimes possible to find a relocated web page by typing in the address of the home page for a website in the URL window of your browser.

Orders: please contact Bookpoint Ltd, 130 Milton Park, Abingdon, Oxon OX14 4SB. Telephone: (44) 01235 827720. Fax: (44) 01235 400454. Lines are open 9.00–17.00, Monday to Saturday, with a 24-hour message answering service. Visit our website at www.hoddereducation.co.uk

© Luke McBratney 2016

First published in 2016 by

Hodder Education

An Hachette UK Company,

Carmelite House, 50 Victoria Embankment

London EC4Y 0DZ

Impression number	5	4	3	2	1
Year	2020	2019	2018	2017	2016

All rights reserved. Apart from any use permitted under UK copyright law, no part of this publication may be reproduced or transmitted in any form or by any means, electronic or mechanical, including photocopying and recording, or held within any information storage and retrieval system, without permission in writing from the publisher or under licence from the Copyright Licensing Agency Limited. Further details of such licences (for reprographic reproduction) may be obtained from the Copyright Licensing Agency Limited, Saffron House, 6–10 Kirby Street, London EC1N 8TS.

Cover photo (and throughout) © 007ea8_930/iStock/Thinkstock/Getty Images

Illustrations by Integra Software Services

Typeset in 11/13pt Univers Lt Std 47 light condensed by Integra Software Services Pvt. Ltd., Pondicherry, India

Printed in Italy

A catalogue record for this title is available from the British Library

ISBN 978 1 4718 5395 1

Contents

Using this guide iv

Introduction ix

1 The poems and poem commentaries 1

   From *Death of a Naturalist* (1966) 1

   From *Door into the Dark* (1969) 6

   From *Wintering Out* (1972) 11

   From *Stations* (1975) 19

   From *North* (1975) 21

   From *Field Work* (1979) 31

   From *Sweeney Astray* (1983) 48

   From *Station Island* (1984) 50

   From *The Haw Lantern* (1987) 60

2 Themes 68

3 The poet's methods 75

4 Contexts 80

5 Working with the text 87

   Assessment Objectives and skills 87

   Building Skills 1: Structuring your writing 90

   Building Skills 2: Analysing texts in detail 97

   Top quotations 100

   Timelines 112

   Map of Ireland 114

   Taking it further 115

Using this guide

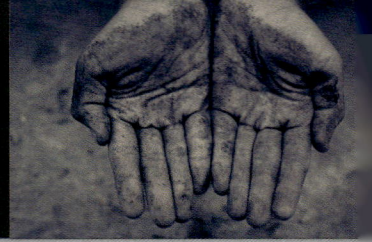

Why read this guide?

The purposes of this A-level Literature Guide are to enable you to organise your thoughts and responses to the text, deepen your understanding of key features and aspects and help you to address the particular requirements of examination questions and Non-exam assessment (NEA) tasks in order to obtain the best possible grade. It will also prove useful to those of you writing an NEA piece on the text as it provides a number of summaries, lists, analyses and references to help with the content and construction of the assignment.

Note that teachers and examiners are seeking above all else evidence of an *informed personal response to the text*. A guide such as this can help you to understand the text, form your own opinions and suggest areas to think about, but it cannot replace your own ideas and responses as an informed and autonomous reader.

Page references in this guide refer to the Faber & Faber edition of *New Selected Poems 1966–1987* (1990). Where a publication is given in the 'Taking it further' section on pages 114–15, the author's surname and publication date only are cited after the first full reference.

How to make the most of this guide

We recommend that you adopt the above advice to your individual reading of the poems. The chapter entitled 'The poems and poem commentaries' helps you to consolidate and extend your own knowledge, as well as offering approaches to analysis and interpretation. After you have formulated an individual response to a poem, you might like to read the relevant poem commentary; or you might like to read a larger section or all the poems, unsupported, before reading the relevant pages of this guide.

The subsequent chapters take a broader view and are designed to enable you to see connections across the whole selection. 'Themes' focuses on how some of the main concerns are explored throughout the poems; 'The poet's methods' considers poetic techniques.

It is vital that you familiarise yourself with the ways your exam board tests your response to the poems. Therefore, use the Specification and the Sample Assessment Materials as your definitive guide to what you need to study and how you are going to be assessed.

Studying Heaney's *New Selected Poems* for A-level

Bear in mind the sort of questions you are going to face in the examination. A-level questions are relatively open, and you have a choice between two. Typically, each one invites you to compare how an aspect — for example, a theme or an idea — is treated in two texts: for AQA specification A, one of the texts is your *New Selected Poems*, the other is your comparative set text: for Eduqas, you compare poems from *Field work* by Heaney to poems from *Skirrid Hill* by Owen Sheers.

Studying Heaney for AS-level

If you are taking WJEC there are two questions on Heaney (the poems from *Field Work* only). The first asks you to write critically about a single poem. The second asks you to compare how a theme or idea is explored in both *Field Work* and in poems from *Skirrid Hill* by Owen Sheers. As part of your preparation, you need to practise analysing each poem as well as comparing themes and ideas that are explored by both Heaney and Sheers. As you do so, you should practise commenting on different viewpoints on the poems. Think of different ways to view each of the poems in class and for yourself, as well as making full use of the critical view features throughout this guide.

Key elements

This guide is designed to help you raise your achievement in your examination response to *New Selected Poems 1966–1987*. It is intended for you to use throughout your AS/A-level English Literature course. It will help you when you are studying the peoms for the first time and also during your revision.

The following features have been used throughout this guide to help you focus your understanding of the peoms:

> **Context**
>
> `Context boxes give contextual evidence that relates directly to particular aspects of the text.`

> **Build critical skills**
>
> Broaden your thinking about the text by answering the questions in the **Build critical skills** boxes. These help you to consider your own opinions in order to develop your skills of criticism and analysis.

> **CRITICAL VIEW**
>
> Critical view boxes highlight a particular critical viewpoint that is relevant to an aspect of the main text. This allows you to develop the higher-level skills needed to come up with your own interpretation of a text.

> **TASK**
>
> **Tasks** are short and focused. They allow you to engage directly with a particular aspect of the text.

Taking it further ▶

Taking it further boxes suggest and provide further background or illuminating parallels to the text.

How to approach the poems

A poem is a heightened rhythmic form of language in which ideas and effects are condensed. The best approach is to allow each poem to reveal itself to you gradually. Work in stages: use close-reading techniques, participate in class discussions and follow up with your own research.

Initial ideas

Begin with an initial reading: read the title and the poem aloud. If possible, hear it: listen to a recording by the poet or an actor and read it aloud yourself.

After a preliminary reading, jot down some initial notes about the poem's overall meaning, but avoid jumping to conclusions; build your response in stages.

Exploring effects

Build on your preliminary ideas by re-reading. Read the poem more slowly. Follow the sense of the poem: when a line is enjambed – that is, it does not end with a punctuation mark – carry on fluently to the next. Be guided by punctuation: if there is a full stop, pause and consider what the sentence has expressed. This close, almost line-by-line approach helps to uncover meaning and allows you to savour poetic effects.

As you re-read, consider the methods the poet uses to shape meaning and create effects. Avoid using a checklist of features to seek in every poem. Allow the poem to suggest which features are of most importance to overall meaning and ideas: here are some suggestions of areas you could consider.

Consider genre – whether the poem is, for instance, a lyric, a dramatic poem or a narrative poem; whether it is a song, a sonnet or a ballad. When you identify a recognisable genre, explore aspects of that genre through further research. For example, having researched the elegy genre, you might consider how a poem like 'The Strand at Lough Beg' uses features of elegy and the extent to which they suit the poem's subject matter and ideas.

Consider form – the poem's shape and the ways in which it is organised. For example, what are the effects of Heaney using a single line stanza at the end of 'Mid-Term Break', a poem otherwise written in tercets?

Consider imagery. How has Heaney used figurative language, personification, symbolism or descriptive language that summons pictures in the reader's mind? For example, how is animal imagery used in poems such as 'The Otter' and 'The Skunk'? To what extent might such uses be tender, admiring or comical and how do they contribute to your overall reading of the poems? In what ways is the harvest bow an important symbol in the poem of that name? Consider the ways in which this symbol gathers significance as the poem progresses and how its meanings and effects contribute to your overall reading of the poem.

Consider aural effects – that is, effects to do with sound. Poems such as 'Death of a Naturalist' and 'Blackberry-Picking' make use of onomatopoeia to evoke aspects of the countryside and childhood experiences. Others, such as 'Punishment' use rhyme and other aural effects, including tone (the tone or mood) but do so less obviously.

The big picture

As you consider what you feel are the most important authorial methods, think about the ways in which these methods work together to shape meaning and create effects. After intense work on the detail of selected features, you should read the poem a final time to unify it and gain a sense of 'the big picture': what the poem's overall concern is, what it is all about.

Using your comparative set text

If you are following the AQA A-level Specification A, you are going to be studying one section of the *New Selected Poems* alongside a comparative set text. As you get to know the themes and ideas in this novel, consider how they are similar to and different from those of the poems you are studying. When something in a poem reminds you of something in your set text, note this comparison and think about how you can explore it. Your comparative set text should give you ideas about your reading of the poems and vice versa.

Introduction

In 1995, Seamus Heaney was awarded the Nobel Prize 'for works of lyrical beauty and ethical depth, which exalt everyday miracles and the living past'. By way of introduction, it is interesting to consider some of the ways in which *New Selected Poems* exemplifies these qualities – qualities that earned him the highest honour in world literature.

In *Death of a Naturalist* the pains of adolescence are evoked in ordinary, rural contexts, but in unusual ways. Blackberries are blood clots, frogs resemble grenades and a spade transforms into a pen. The living past is evoked through rural work in *Door into the Dark* poems such as 'Thatcher' and 'The Wife's Tale', and there is ethical depth in the handling of Irish political struggle in 'Requiem for the Croppies'. This is also true of *Wintering Out* and the increasingly complex poems that use the Irish landscape to explore politics and Irish identity, through poems like 'Broagh' and 'Anahorish'. Bodies of Iron Age sacrifices surface as arresting images with uncomfortable parallels to 1970s Northern Ireland, and poems such as 'The Tollund Man' come to exemplify what Heaney meant when he said he sought 'images and symbols adequate to our predicament' (Seamus Heaney, *Preoccupations*, London: Faber & Faber, 1984, p.56).

Much of *North* is in that vein. 'Punishment', for example, displays ethical depth in its willingness to confront uncomfortable feelings in response to a Catholic being publicly humiliated by her own community for sleeping with a British soldier. The ways in which Heaney addresses the conflict are varied. 'Act of Union' re-imagines an 1800 Act of Parliament as an abusive relationship which produces an illegitimate child (Northern Ireland). He also explores how Catholics and Protestants interact and the tiny level of distance and reserve present in poems like 'The Other Side'.

Field Work offers escape in its evocation of country life in Glanmore, County Wicklow and it contains some beautiful love poetry. The ugliness of conflict is also rendered in language of lyrical beauty. 'The Strand at Lough Beg' uses pastoral imagery and references to Dante to elegise Heaney's second cousin who was murdered in a random sectarian attack. In the final lines, the speaker washes his relative's wounds with morning dew as he prepares him for the next life.

In *Station Island* a tougher attitude emerges. In these dramatic poems, a pilgrimage intended to offer rest and renewal is disturbed by religious doubts and by ghosts from the past. For example, the murdered relative from 'The Strand at Lough Beg' arises and castigates the poet directly, accusing him of confusing 'evasion and artistic tact'. But, by the end of the sequence there is a renewal of sorts, and, in the voice of Sweeney, the seventh-century Ulster king, Heaney hits back at his critics for their jealousy and pettiness and realises (with typical understatement) his 'not inconsiderable contribution' to their art.

In *The Haw Lantern* the lessons learnt are put into practice. The work is still recognisably Irish, but has a broader, international reach. Satire and humour are in greater evidence as is a loss of faith in both religion and country. Poems such as 'From the Republic of Conscience' and in 'The Mud Vision' dazzle with their strangeness and reflect on the state of the poet's nation.

While such public poems are prominent, others spring from personal concerns. Of particular lyrical beauty are the 'Clearances' sonnets for Heaney's dead mother. Indeed, explorations of Heaney's family life and the places of his boyhood have been present in every collection: from the poems for his sons and for his daughter in *Station Island* to 'Sunlight' from *North* – a tender poem for Heaney's aunt that renders everyday work as miraculous.

The depth and complexity of Heaney's verse means that both close reading and re-reading are richly rewarded. Such qualities also mean that *New Selected Poems* is an ideal comparative text. With a richness both textual and contextual, it engages with literature, politics, history, society, identity and many other issues in subtle and surprising ways. And while Heaney's subject matter might typically be rooted in Irish concerns, the scope of his poetry is universal.

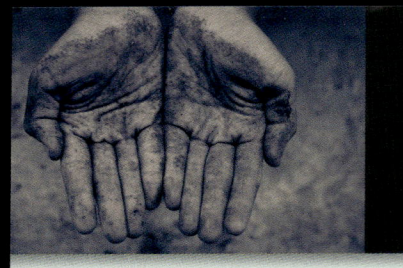

The poems and poem commentaries

Target your thinking

- What is your considered personal response to the poem – what do you think are its main concerns or ideas? (**AO1**)
- What other interpretations might you offer? (**AO5**)
- Which are the most important methods used in the poem: how does Heaney use them to shape meaning and create effects? (**AO2**)
- How is the meaning of the poem shaped by your understanding of its contexts? (**AO3**)
- In what ways can you connect the poem's themes, ideas or methods to other poems in the selection, or to your comparative set text? (**AO4**)

From *Death of a Naturalist* (1966)

In **'Digging'**, the speaker turns from contemplating the pen in his hand to look out of the window at his father digging. This action releases memories of both his father and his grandfather. He vows to dig with his pen rather than the spade. The speaker in **'Follower'** remembers his father's prowess as a ploughman and how he used to follow him around the farm, yet realises that now his father is the one who follows him. In **'Blackberry-Picking'** happy childhood memories are replaced by adolescent horror when the berries rot. Similarly, **'Death of a Naturalist'** shows how, in time, delightful frogspawn transforms sickeningly into threatening frogs. Death of a literal kind intrudes in **'Mid-Term Break'** when the speaker returns from boarding school to attend his brother's funeral. **'Poem'** is both a love poem for Heaney's wife and a statement of poetic intent; he will improve himself for her, and she will support his poetic vocation. Dedicated to fellow poet Michael Longley, **'Personal Helicon'** uses a childhood fascination with wells and pumps as a metaphor for poetic inspiration and creation.

Commentary 'Digging' was the first poem that Heaney wrote where he thought his 'feelings had got into words' or where his *feel* had got into words'. He 'had let down a shaft into real life' (Heaney 1984, p.41), and – as with other poems in *Death of a Naturalist* – reality is evoked through vivid sensuous details. Sounds of the 'clean rasping' as his father's 'spade sinks into gravelly ground' cause the speaker to turn from his creative work and consider the manual labour of digging. Note how a chorus of aural effects brings the

Onomatopoeia: the use of a word that suggests or imitates the sound it refers to, such as boom or plop.

experience alive: think, for example, of the **onomatopoeia** in 'rasping', the sound evoked by the spade penetrating the 'gravelly ground', the alliterated 'g' sounds, the sibilance and the full rhyme.

Consider how the experience is structured. The focus shifts from the speaker's creative work to a contemplation of his father's digging, which releases the memory of his father digging and scattering potatoes, which he and others (possibly his siblings) would collect. Note how the past is every bit as alive as the present. In the fourth stanza the descriptions are vivid, and a plethora of active verbs – such as 'levered', 'rooted', 'buried' and 'scatter' – evoke the father's industry and precision. 'The coarse boot nestled' seems paradoxical – we don't expect a rough work boot to be followed by a word with connotations of domesticity – but Heaney's speaker is expressing admiration for a father whose work not only demands strength but is also carried out with precision and care; the delight of his children in working with him is evident as they gather the potatoes that he digs: 'Loving their cool hardness in our hands'.

After an awestruck statement about his father's skills, thoughts of his grandfather's digging release another memory, this one as vivid as the first.

The meditation on digging releases a truth about his present situation. Coming full circle, the poem returns to a close up of the speaker's pen. The first line and a half of the final stanza are exactly the same as those of the first, but the memories experienced have produced a new certainty in the speaker. He makes a vow about what he will do with his pen, the conclusiveness and importance of which are underscored by it being given a line of its own, the shortest in the poem: 'I'll dig with it.'

CRITICAL VIEW

In an essay entitled 'Feeling into Words', Heaney offers a view of poetry which is influenced by the Romantic poet William Wordsworth:

'poetry as divination, poetry as revelation of the self to the self, a restoration of the culture to itself, poems as elements of continuity, with the aura and authenticity of archaeological finds, where the buried shard has an importance that is not diminished by the importance of the buried city; poetry as a dig, a dig for finds that end up being plants.'

(Heaney, 1984, p.41)

The poem, then, is about trying to keep faith with the past while breaking from that past; while physically looking down on his father as he digs, the poet is at pains not to take the high ground as an intellectual and look down metaphorically on the manual work done by his forebears. Heaney has written about the origins of the pen/spade metaphor, citing sayings from his childhood which were meant to encourage study – '"learning's easy carried" and "the pen's lighter than the spade". And the poem does no more than allow that bud

The poems and poem commentaries

of wisdom to exfoliate' (Heaney 1984, p.42). **'Digging'** is interesting too for the ways in which it deals with issues that are important in Heaney's work as a whole, such as fathers and sons, identity, the rural landscape and work, memory, childhood and poetry itself. Some find hints of the violence that Heaney will explore later in his career in the 'snug as a gun' simile of the first stanza; similar hints are contained through the **semantic field** of conflict in **'Death of a Naturalist'** through words such as 'invaded', 'cocked' and 'mud grenades'.

Whether you agree with Heaney that the gun image is about 'the connection between the "uh" sounds in "thumb" and "snug" and "gun" that are the heart of the poetic subject matter rather than any sociological or literary formation' (Dennis O'Driscoll, *Stepping Stones*, Farrar, Straus and Giroux: New York, 2008, pp.82–3), or if you see a subliminal image of the violence that was to break out in the Northern Ireland conflict, such details show that, for Heaney, the Irish countryside is much more than a **pastoral** idyll.

There is certainly an anti-pastoral strain in other poems from *Death of a Naturalist*. In **'Personal Helicon'**, the rat which 'slapped across' the speaker's reflection in his youth perhaps suggests troubling aspects of the psyche that might be uncovered when deep in poetic meditation as well as avoiding presenting the countryside as being uncomplicatedly benign.

Semantic field: a group of words linked by their meaning.

Pastoral: a text that contains idealised images of the countryside.

> ### Context
>
> ```
> 'Personal Helicon''s title refers to Helicon, the mountain
> in Greece where the goddesses of the arts and sciences were
> said to live. The muse, or muses, are often used as a term
> for creative inspiration; sometimes a particular person -
> often a loved one - is said to be a muse. How is Heaney's
> muse presented in 'Personal Helicon'?
> ```

This is also the case in **'Death of a Naturalist'** and **'Blackberry-Picking'**. Both poems have a bipartite (two-part) structure: the first **verse paragraph** narrates a table of innocence; the second, one of experience.

In both parts, dense sensuous language is used to evoke the experiences and the experience part of each poem the language presents simultaneously the discomfort of the incident described and the pains of growing up. For example, in **'Blackberry-Picking'** the speaker 'always felt like crying' because the 'fruit fermented [and] the sweet flesh would turn sour' and, in **'Death of a Naturalist'**, the 'angry frogs' invade and their 'coarse croaking' forms a threatening 'bass chorus'. The changing nature of the blackberries is analogous to the changing nature of the body through puberty, and the deep and croaking noise the frogs make is reminiscent of a boy's voice breaking and deepening during adolescence. Heaney himself has emphasised the way in which his early poems explore the explosive impact of burgeoning sexuality: 'those mud

Verse paragraph: a group of several lines in a poem that make up a narrative unit, in a similar way to a paragraph in prose.

grenades in "Death of a Naturalist" … seem to have a sexual pin in them just waiting to be pulled' (O'Driscoll 2008, p.83).

While the poems chart a course from innocence to experience, Heaney does not present these states as simple binary opposites: the seeds of experience are sown in innocence. For example, **'Death of a Naturalist'** opens with 'All year the flax-dam festered in the heart/ Of the townland'; note how the verb 'festered' — something that we associate with infected wounds or leaking pus — is positioned prominently in the middle of the line, with a stress on its first syllable and an 'f' that alliterates with the first syllable of 'flax-dam'. Similarly, the first verse paragraph of **'Blackberry-Picking'** contains troubling elements: the first blackberry, for example, is described as a coagulation of blood: 'a glossy purple clot'. And the transformations that adolescence will effect are foreshadowed in the way the children's desire to pick is rendered as 'lust' and in the more dark imagery at the end of stanza where their 'palms [are as] sticky as Bluebeard's'. This alludes to 'Bluebeard', the fairy story by Charles Perrault in which the eponymous character murdered his wives for entering a forbidden room, but might also carry connotations of masturbation.

Changes beyond adolescence are also charted. **'Follower'** explores the shift in a father and son relationship, **'Poem'** contemplates changes through marriage and **'Mid-Term Break'** explores death. Based on the death of Heaney's younger brother, Christopher, 'Mid-Term Break' is reminiscent of the early writing of James Joyce, whose collection of stories *Dubliners* is written in a style of 'scrupulous meanness' and without authorial comment.

The experience of returning from school to attend the funeral is narrated simply in a linear narrative from the child speaker's perspective. Note the foreshadowing in the first stanza: the place of waiting is associated with illness ('sick bay'), there is a sense of things coming 'to a close' and bells are 'knelling' (a verb we associate with funeral bells). A sense of the strangeness of the experience is conveyed in the second stanza through the meeting his 'father crying', and, like the poem's title, the words of Big Jim Evans have a double meaning: 'a hard blow' suggests both an emotional hurt and the impact of the car that hit his brother.

Information is revealed gradually, and the poem closes on images of the dead boy's room before concluding with the accident and a poignant stanza — 'A four foot box, a foot for every year' — which stands out owing to it being a single line stanza in a poem of **tercets**.

Perhaps the stanza being cut short suggests the life that has been cut short. Its full rhyme (in an otherwise unrhymed poem) encourages the reader to dwell on its image of the coffin, the detail of the accident — 'the bumper knocked him clear' — and on the dead boy's age: only four years old.

Changes brought by marriage are evoked in **'Poem'**, which is dedicated to Heaney's wife. The first and final stanzas begin with a word that is rare in Heaney's oeuvre: 'Love'. Obviously there is the colloquial sense of his wife

---

Taking it further ▶

Read 'The Sisters', the first story from *Dubliners* by James Joyce. Compare the ways in which a child's first experience of death is presented in the story and in 'Mid-Term Break'.

TASK

What meanings might the expression 'Mid-Term Break' have? In what ways is this an appropriate title for the poem?

Tercet: a stanza of three lines.

being called 'love', but perhaps there is also the sense that, to him, she is the very personification of that quality. Images of setting limits are at the heart of the poem: the child-speaker's ineffectual attempts to perform rural work, such as keeping out livestock or holding back water from a drain are rendered in a tone of gentle amusement. Yet the final stanza grows more tender and serious as his wife helps him to work within 'new limits' and 'arrange the world'. It concludes with his wife providing a solution to the seemingly intractable: she will 'arrange the world/ And square the circle: four walls and a ring'. Note the play on words, with walls for square and ring for circle as well as the wedding ring. On one level, the poem might be seen as one-sided: these are all the things that marriage is going to do for him: she is going to preserve his creativity – his inner child – and expand his horizons by taking a traditional domestic role as the married woman within the confines of the four walls of their home. Yet the poem is also touchingly self-deprecating in its portrayal of the childishly ineffectual attempts to perform common tasks – which are perhaps analogous to attempts to write formal verse – and it also lends weight to the importance of his wife in his future success. Before her, he was only able to work within 'small imperfect limits [which] would keep breaking'; with her, his limits are those of 'the world'.

Breaking away from limits and traditions are important elements of *Death of a Naturalist*, and there is a sense not only of the respect for ancient crafts and labour, but also of them becoming obsolete. Just as the speaker in 'Digging' will never wield a spade in the way his forefathers did, he will never be a ploughman like the father in **'Follower'**. The idea of following in one's father's footsteps is treated ironically here and the fall from innocence to experience is perhaps – with the exception of 'Mid-Term Break' – the hardest. Note how the shift in point of view suggests the shift in the father–son relationship: the first three quatrains are in the third person, with the father – a kind of **Atlas**-figure of strength to his boy – being remembered and admired; the last three stanzas are in first person as the thoughts and feelings of the son (now a man) take centre stage.

At first, there is self-awareness: the boy recognises how he was 'a nuisance', but the final shift in tone and to the present tense is abrupt, harsh and painfully honest:

> … But today
> It is my father who keeps stumbling
> Behind me, and will not go away

The poet who vowed to dig with his pen and who 'rhyme[s]/ To see [himself]', has dug into the depths of his feelings, uncovered a difficult truth about the changing dynamic in parent–child relationships and has had the courage to express this honestly, simply and – for the reader – heart-breakingly. Avoiding a sentimental portrayal of the changes in familial roles, Heaney shows courage in confronting moral complexities and is true to what people really feel, rather than what they think they ought to feel. It is a feature of his writing that we shall see in his later collections.

Atlas: a figure in Greek mythology who held up the heavens; he is often depicted as supporting a globe on his shoulders.

Taking it further ▶

If you are studying AQA English Literature Specification A, compare the ways in which aspects of growing up are presented in the poems by Heaney and in your novel, for example, Michael Frayn's *Spies*, Jeanette Winterson's *Oranges Are Not the Only Fruit* or Graham Swift's *Waterland*.

From *Door into the Dark* (1969)

From the confines of family and the parish of Mossbawn in *Death of a Naturalist*, *Door into the Dark* travels into wider spaces. It is, as Blake Morrison notes, 'a less fearful collection' than its predecessor, 'one more willing to acknowledge the fascination of darkness.' (Blake Morrison, *Seamus Heaney*, London: Methuen, 1982).

Darkness and travelling are marked features of poems such as **'The Peninsula'** and **'Night Drive'**. In the former, a drive along the Ards Peninsula in County Down is taken as a cure for writer's block, and in the latter the drive is through France to meet his wife in Italy. Both convey a pleasure in the action of driving and movement. In **'The Peninsula'** there is a kind of meditative pleasure in passing through a changing landscape – and one that comes alive in a different way upon reflection; in **'Night Drive'** the speaker's anticipation of his love-making is suggested by the features on the landscape as he journeys south. **'Thatcher'** and **'The Wife's Tale'** both document rural work. The title character in **'Thatcher'** arrives unexpectedly and seems to take all morning preparing for work, but his craftsmanship is impressive and leaves people awestruck when the new roof is complete. Told in the voice of the wife of a farmer, who brings refreshments to her husband and his workers during a break from threshing, 'The Wife's Tale' evokes a way of life and a marriage. **'Relic of Memory'** marvels at a scientific exhibit displayed in the classroom in Anahorish school: a piece of wood that has been petrified (turned into stone) in the waters of Lough Neagh (the large freshwater lake in the middle of Northern Ireland).

In *Door into the Dark*, Heaney moves outwards towards areas that will continue to preoccupy him in later collections. In **'Requiem for the Croppies'** he narrates the experience of the men who fought in the United Irishmen's uprising in 1798 (see Contexts, p.82). They were a band of ill-equipped fighters from all sections of their communities, who faced British cannon, died and were buried without funeral rites. **'Bogland'** also speaks of Ireland from the perspective of a whole people, contrasting the Irish landscape with that of America and characterising the Irish bog as a magical place that contains layers of history and as a natural poetic territory.

Commentary Like earlier poems, such as 'Digging' and 'Follower', **'Thatcher'** evokes rural work and traditions, though this time outside of the family context. Note the way in which respect for the thatcher builds as the poem progresses: at first he is characterised by his unpredictability – he turns up 'unexpectedly'; his equipment seems minimal – his bicycle is 'slung/ With a light ladder and a bag of knives' and when he begins work, nothing seems to happen for hours – 'It seemed he spent the morning warming up'. Yet there is a shift in mood in the second half of the poem as the work is depicted as masterful – magical even. With a high concentration of active verbs, the speaker details the work and then precise descriptions give way to metaphor and allusion at the end of the poem

> **Taking it further** ▶
>
> See Heaney discuss the reception of 'Requiem for the croppies' in this clip from the BBC: www.bbc.co.uk/education/clips/zqnd7ty

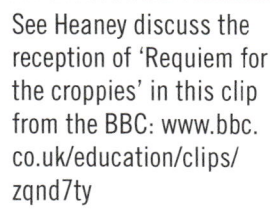

The poems and poem commentaries

to convey a sense of wonder: the roof is transformed 'into a sloped honeycomb' and the family gape at the thatcher's 'Midas touch'.

Note the use of vocabulary suggesting skill and power: what were a 'bag of knives' in the first quatrain become 'well-honed blades' in the third, the Old English verb 'honed' evoking comparisons with sharpened weapons; the final quatrain begins with the heraldic term 'couchant', suggesting the thatcher lies like a lion — perhaps with latent power.

It would, however, be wrong to suggest that Heaney is simply in awe; there is a subtle distance between the events and the speaker who describes them. The whole poem is in the third person and the final line, which evokes the magic of the thatcher's craft and the effect it has on those watching, excludes the poet: it 'left *them* gaping at his Midas touch' (my emphasis). Heaney depicts rural customs, but it might seem that he is no longer fully part of them.

'The Wife's Tale' achieves distance from the poet by being a dramatic monologue in the persona of a farmer's wife who brings tea to her husband and his workers. The events of the poem take place during an important time in the farming calendar: threshing, which is the process of removing the edible part of the corn (the seed) from the inedible parts. Like many of the narrative poems of Robert Frost, there are detailed descriptions of the rural setting but few of the main characters, leaving it to the reader to consider just what sort of a story is being told.

Many regard the poem as being primarily concerned with the relationship between the husband and wife, with Michael Parker seeing a 'pairing of a sensitive wife and an unsympathetic husband/ "master"' (Michael Parker, *Seamus Heaney: The Making of the Poet,* London: Gill and Macmillan,1993, pp.80–1). The husband might be seen as being dismissive of his wife's contributions and ordering her to do things, such as 'Give these fellows theirs' and 'Away over there and look'. Parker also suggests that Heaney's recent marriage 'had perhaps sensitized Heaney' to gender inequalities – 'the fate of his own mother and to that of millions of women.' (p.80). This reading suggests that the dramatic monologue form enables the poet to 'distance himself from the male complacency he depicts and perhaps shared'.

Yet this is not the only way to read the poem. While the last stanza shows a clear demarcation of gender roles, which excludes the wife – 'I'd come and he had shown me/ So I belonged no further to the work' – it is possible to detect a more loving marriage being depicted. The farmer's first speech is presumably in response to his wife serving him first and him being thoughtful towards his workers. A good threshing day depends on gaining good work from the labourers, and his wife bringing tea is likely to build morale – an important aspect in gaining the most from the men. The farmer doesn't take his wife's work for granted; he compliments her on laying out the spread: 'That looks well', he says, appreciating that she has gone to extra trouble. His joking comment about

Taking it further ▶

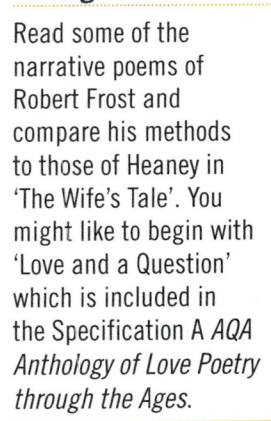

Read some of the narrative poems of Robert Frost and compare his methods to those of Heaney in 'The Wife's Tale'. You might like to begin with 'Love and a Question' which is included in the Specification A *AQA Anthology of Love Poetry through the Ages.*

'boys like us have little call for cloths' reduces social distance, amusing the men and building camaraderie between boss and workers. Note how 'He winked, then watched me'; a wink is usually a gesture between two people suggesting a shared secret, or that the remark made should not be taken seriously. It might show intimacy between the husband and wife, while suggesting that he *is* actually pleased to enjoy his tea served on a cloth. Even the way in which the wife 'buttered the thick slices that he likes' might be seen to show her taking pleasure in providing her husband with what he wants. His invitation to her to inspect the seed perhaps shows him wanting her to take pleasure in his work – perhaps he is demonstrating his power to provide; the corn that has been planted and cared for has finally borne fruit. A good or bad threshing day could make the difference between having sufficient means to survive and having the means to enjoy some luxuries. Even if the wife doesn't know what she's looking for, she still lingers on the task, sensuously enjoying feeling the contents of the bags: her husband's seed is 'hard as shot,/ Innumerable and cool'.

The poem's conclusion might be read as the wife being distanced from the world of the men, as she goes about clearing up, resentfully, while they relax. However, it could be argued that the poem depicts a marriage in which there are two different, but complementary roles. Heaney himself has said that the poem addresses itself to 'the balance between man and woman' (quoted in Parker 1993, p.80). Balance implies both equality and difference. Hence, the final lines might depict this balance. The men, who have just been working on the exhausting task of threshing, 'still kept their ease/ Spread out, unbuttoned, grateful, under the trees.' The final full rhyme sounds a note of satisfaction, and – like the earlier description of the buttering of the bread – there is a sense of contentment in bringing pleasure to others. Note how the last adjective in the final line's tripartite list – 'grateful' – refers to the appreciation the men have for their rest and refreshment.

Love and marriage are also presented in **'Night Drive'**, which is set in continental Europe as the speaker drives to Italy to join his wife. Consider how Heaney uses sensuous language to evoke the smells, sights and sounds along the way and how he uses descriptions of the journey to suggest sexual feelings. Driving is also the action taking place in **'The Peninsula'**; writer's block causes the speaker to go for a drive along the Ards Peninsula (the landmass to the east of Strangford Lough). At first the landscape seems secondary to the act of driving. 'The sky is tall as over a runway', land is 'without marks' and 'the whitewashed gable' disappears into a field as darkness falls; Heaney uses impersonal images and wrong-foots the reader who might have been expecting a glorious scene to elevate and inspire the speaker. Yet the second part of the poem conveys the power of the landscape and that of memory as the speaker returns at night, remembering the details of the earlier drive. Note how the details now spring to life: whereas the dusky horizons previously drank 'down sea and hill', now he recalls 'That rock where breakers shredded into

The poems and poem commentaries

rags' and 'The leggy birds stilted on their own legs'. Despite the speaker later saying he drives home 'still with nothing to say', it seems that through such vivid and specific figurative language his poetic imagination *has* been fired by the landscape. The final part of the poem expands on the significance of the experience: all landscapes will be uncoded by this – 'things founded clean on their own shapes,/ Water and ground in their extremity'.

Water is an awesome natural phenomenon in this collection. In **'Relic of Memory'** it is a preserver of ambiguous curiosities. Note the effects of Heaney's use of paradox and the way in which rhyme reinforces the connections between the items that went into the water and what they transformed into: the 'oars and posts ... Incarcerate ghosts'; 'The cooling star ... Of burnt meteor'. Yet the biggest sense of wonder is reserved for the climactic image:

> That relic stored –
> A piece of stone
> On the shelf at school,
> Oatmeal coloured.

The concluding poem of *Door into the Dark*, **'Bogland'**, celebrates the watery landscape and its sense of endless potential, using the bog as a metaphor for the bottomless well of the imagination. The poem moves from vast exterior spaces – the landscape of the American prairies – to dig down into the 'wet centre' of the Irish bogs and shows that a pioneer is not necessarily one who heads west to settle in new lands like the American pioneers of the nineteenth century. Heaney is addressing exploration of a different sort: 'Our pioneers keep striking/ Inwards and downwards'. Unlike the American pioneers, who settled in virgin territory, 'Every layer' Ireland's pioneers 'strip/ Seems camped on before'. In other words, the bog preserves not only things, but layers of Irish history and culture. A sense of shared heritage is also suggested by Heaney's chosen point of view: as he does in **'Requiem for the Croppies'** (see the Working with the text section on p.97), his speaker uses the first person plural, seemingly speaking for his nation as much as for himself.

While bogland might be considered unpleasant by some – expressions containing bog are often associated with backwardness and an unsophisticated rural lifestyle, with, for example, country people being dismissed as bogtrotters and Gaelic football as bogball – in **'Bogland'**, the bog is a place of infinite wonder.

The skeleton of the Great Irish Elk is 'astounding' when exhibited, and well-preserved, century-old butter provides a homely contrast to this impressive archaeological discovery that leads the speaker to a find a metaphor for the land's sensuous goodness: 'The ground itself is kind, black butter/ Melting and opening underfoot'. On one level, then, this is a poem of reclamation: the peat

Build critical skills

What are the effects of the fossil being called a 'relic'? Explain the significance of the title, 'Relic of Memory'.

TASK

Heaney says of his title to the collection, 'I intended to gesture towards this idea of poetry as a point of entry into the buried life of the feelings or as a point of exit for it' (Heaney 1984, p.52). Explain Heaney's statement by referring to examples from the *Door into the Dark*.

bog is a place worthy of our interest and exploration. On another, it is a poem of dedication. Not only does Heaney dedicate it to his friend, the painter T.P. Flanagan, showing a personal and shared engagement with the subject matter, but also he seems to dedicate himself to exploring the bog and by extension Ireland – its myths, its culture, its history. His seriousness of purpose to this task can be seen in abundance in his next two collections, *Wintering Out* and *North*.

▲ The 1967 painting 'Boglands (for Seamus Heaney)' by T.P. Flanagan from the 'Gortahork' sequence

Context

'By the late 1960s, a strong friendship had been formed between the Flanagan and Heaney families, and the 1967 painting "Boglands (for Seamus Heaney)", part of the powerful "Gortahork" sequence, resulted in the complementary poem, "Bogland: for T.P. Flanagan", as a kind of inspiring and affectionate interchange of ideas (and dedications) came into play.'

(The *Independent*, Monday 18 April 2011)

The poems and poem commentaries

> **Context**
>
> ```
> In an essay entitled 'Feeling into Words' Heaney recalls
> how, when he was a young boy, adults 'put it about (and we
> believed them) that there was no bottom in the bog-holes'
> (Heaney 1984, p.56). In another essay, 'Mossbawn', Heaney
> writes how boggy places hold an 'immediate and deeply
> peaceful attraction' for him; it is as if he is 'betrothed
> to them'. He believes this 'brethothal happened' when he
> and another boy 'bathed in a moss-hole, treading the liver-
> thick mud, unsettling a smoky muck off the bottom and
> coming out smeared and weedy and darkened … [and] somehow
> initiated' (Heaney 1984, p.19).
> ```

From *Wintering Out* (1972)

Many of the poems use the Irish landscape. In a similar way to his memory of being immersed in the muddy waters of the bog as a boy, in **'Oracle'** Heaney explores closeness to the landscape by enacting a childhood memory — this time, of hiding inside the trunk of a willow tree. The landscape is also a means for him to explore wider issues such as Irish identity, colonialism and contemporary politics. **'Bog Oak'**, for example, begins with a meditation on a piece of oak recovered from a peat bog (which was the typical building material of the Irish), but becomes a consideration of conquest as the speaker imagines the English poet, Edmund Spenser, who was part of the Plantation of Ulster yet able to remain aloof from the Irish people, ignoring their starvation and poverty. **'Anahorish'** and **'Broagh'** explore place names, with the former offering images of both the 'place of clear water' and its early inhabitants and 'Broagh' offering imagery of a damaged Eden and a glimpse of those who occupied it but found its Irish name difficult to pronounce.

As its title suggests, **'Gifts of Rain'** is concerned with what rain gives to the land. An arresting poem, it is full of unusual watery images, though it does not reveal obvious meanings easily. It is divided into four sections: the first describes the actions of a mammal — perhaps a hedgehog — during a downpour; the second, a man groping in drenched soil as he checks on seeds he has planted; the third introduces the poetic speaker as he hears the sounds of the river; and the fourth relates to that river as a goddess. The introduction of the speaker perhaps lends the imagery more concrete meaning; the poem seems to be calling on powers of the river to heal and cleanse. The speaker looks back at those who have peacefully given their lives to uniting Ireland and the water imagery might suggest that the landscape is being called upon to cleanse and purge and perhaps offer the troubled country a new beginning.

NEW SELECTED POEMS 1966–1987

> **TASK**
>
> When Heaney wrote the first line of 'The Tollund Man' – a poem he regards as 'the first fruits' of his reading of Glob – he felt the 'aura surrounding' the head of the preserved body, an experience that was 'uncanny in the full technical sense' (O'Driscoll 2008, p.124; p.157). By close reference to the poem explain what you think Heaney means.

Taking it further ▶

Look up the term 'uncanny' in a good dictionary of literary terms. You might also like to search on the internet for an influential essay by Sigmund Freud entitled 'The Uncanny' (1919). In what ways does knowing more about the uncanny help you to appreciate uncanny effects in Heaney's poetry?

'The Tollund Man' is one of the famous poems in which Heaney uses imagery suggested by the discovery of ancient bodies preserved in peat bogs. The speaker is an overt presence in the poem, vowing to go to the Jutland in Denmark to see the body that became known as the Tollund Man (after the village nearest to his discovery). The parallels between death through an Iron Age sacrifice in Denmark and the those who die as a consequence of the conflict in Northern Ireland become clear as the poem continues; when the speaker journeys to the Jutland he will feel unhappy at the deaths of the sacrificed people, but also 'at home'.

> **Context**
>
> Heaney was inspired to write about bodies preserved in peat bogs through his reading *The Bog People* by the archaeologist P. V. Glob. He describes opening this book as being like 'opening a gate, the same as when I wrote "Bogland"' (O'Driscoll 2008, p.157). For more information on Glob and the effects of his book on Heaney's work, see pp.24–5 and p.81 of this guide.

'A New Song' incorporates elements of English and Gaelic traditions into a love poem that attempts to build bridges between both cultures. **'Wedding Day'** is an autobiographical poem that recalls Heaney's wedding day, but remembers the anxieties of this public event, which only seem to dissipate when he is alone with his wife and asks to sleep on her breast as they drive towards their honeymoon. In another domestic lyric, **'Summer Home'**, five stages of experiencing and overcoming discord in marriage unfold. The unnamed difficulty is evoked in Section I. In Section II, the wife's weeping causes the husband to accept blame; in Section III, the couple make love in an attempt to overcome their difficulties. Section IV presents sexual climax, yet, at the start of Section V, the crying of the couple's children suggests that all is not healed. The image that concludes the poem is more hopeful: though the sound of their love is tiny, it can be heard with the clarity of a tuning fork.

'Limbo' and **'Bye-Child'** narrate stories of unwanted children: the former an illegitimate boy drowned by a mother who couldn't keep him; the latter a boy who had been confined by his mother to a hen house. While **'Limbo'** concludes with imagery that suggests that the child unwanted in this life remains untouchable in the next – since medieval Catholic doctrine once decreed that the unbaptised must remain in a place called Limbo, rather than be eligible for heaven – **'Bye-Child'** concludes with hints of recovery as the neglected boy begins to speak. **'Westering'** concludes the collection with a sense of journey, but with more than a backward glance. An image of the moon, on a map in California, leads the speaker to remember the moonlight falling on the cobbles of the yard in a house in Donegal and then to recall his feelings as he drove away on Good Friday, having missed the usual religious observances.

The poems and poem commentaries

Commentary 'Oracle', which expresses intimacy with the landscape to the point that it is an extension of the speaker rather than something external, is written in the second person, placing the reader in the perspective of the little boy who hides in the tree trunk and becomes a spirit of the willow. The poem has elements of the shape poem – on the page, it resembles a tree trunk visually – and the sonnet – it is a love poem to nature in 14 lines. In the 'woody cleft' the child's sense of hearing is heightened. He hears minute details like his parents' drawing 'the poles of stiles' and their call is experienced in terms of nature and evoked through onomatopoeia as 'they/ cuckoo your name' (presumably evoking the soft calling of the bisyllabic name Seamus). At the end of the poem, the boy has almost become part of the tree: his ear and voice are 'lobe and larynx/ of the mossy places'. Perhaps the implication is that the child's poetic vocation is announced; in this pastoral context, the speaker is reduced to the two body parts essential for a career in verse: the ear (to hear the stories of his landscape and his people), and the voice (to articulate his poetic thoughts and feelings).

Such ideas are also apparent in **'Gifts of Rain'**. The 'Soundings' of the first section might be thought of as the creature attuning itself to the land, perhaps symbolic of Heaney attuning himself to his landscape and his people. In section three, the speaker listens overtly to the sounds of the rain. Note the plethora of effects that bring the rains to life. First they are **anthropomorphised** into a group of people at a 'gathering'. Their 'all-night/ roaring' suggests a raucous, long party, with the onomatopoeia ('roaring') enhancing the sense of the loudness. Repeated 'r' sounds run through the next few stanzas until the noise shifts through more onomatopoeia to a more ugly, or drunken-sounding, 'slabbering' before we hear of the River Moyola 'harping on/ its gravel beds'. This last sound is ambiguous, both elevating the river and bringing it back down to earth, since 'harping on' evokes both the beautiful sound of the Irish national instrument (which is often used as a symbol for the country) and the idiom for complaining. The poem's perspective moves from third to first person as the poetic speaker intrudes and listens to the music of the River Moyola (which runs through County Derry to Lough Neagh and is the river Heaney remembers from his childhood). It seems that, as in 'Oracle', the speaker is turning to the local landscape for insight and guidance. The 'shared calling of blood' and the 'Soft voices of the dead' may represent the people in the past who died for Ireland, but the language is sufficiently open to allow the reader to ponder the significance. Just as 'Oracle' was titled to encourage the reader to think that there was something mystical in the landscape that could pass on divine – but perhaps cryptic – advice, in 'Gifts of Rain' nature gives something mysterious but important. In the final section, Heaney punningly evokes the river's attractive sounds. A 'score' is a musical composition, and 'consort' makes the reader think of a concert of music (as well as perhaps a companion, as in a consort). The noise of the river has grown softer than in the previous section. Note the excess of vowel sounds and the easy sibilance as the river is rendered as a type

> **Taking it further** ▶
>
> Heaney has said of 'Oracle': 'I remember much of my childhood as a trance of loneliness, and in those places something in me was utterly at peace' (O'Driscoll 2008, p.264) and that '"Oracle" is more Thomasy than Frosty, more English-naturey than than Frost' (O'Driscoll 2008, p.454.) How might these references help you to further appreciate Heaney's work?

anthropomorphism: the giving of human characteristics or behaviours to nature, animals, gods or things.

> **TASK**
>
> Find out more about the work of the poets Edward Thomas and Robert Frost. You might begin by considering well-known poems such as 'The Manor Farm' and 'Adlestrop' by Thomas and 'Stopping by Woods on a Snowy Evening' and 'The Road Not Taken' by Frost.

NEW SELECTED POEMS 1966–1987

> **TASK**
> Consider the ways in which the river as a female is used in the poem. What effects does it have on the speaker?

of woodwind instrument – 'an old chanter/ breathing its mists/ through vowels and history'. The river also takes on sexual connotations as the speaker hears its 'mating call of sound' and feels it rising 'to pleasure' him. There is a sense that a close identification with the landscape will bring fulfilment and perhaps unite warring elements together: the river is a 'hoarder of common ground'.

> **Context**
>
> To present aspects of the landscape as female is common in literature. In Irish literature there is also a genre of poetry known as the **aisling** in which a vision of Ireland appears as a woman. Often this female figure laments the state of the country and predicts a revival of its fortunes. Aisling (pronounced ASH-ling) is also a popular a girl's name in Ireland.

Prelapsarian: (from the Bible) at a time, before the Fall, when Adam and Eve were innocent and without sin in the Garden of Eden. By extension, unspoilt, pure and innocent.

The landscape is a source of comfort and inspiration in a different way in the place-name poems **'Anahorish'** and **'Broagh'**. Written in the Irish *dinnseanchas* tradition (in which the name of the place encapsulates aspects of the character of that place), the poems are simultaneously personal and public: Anahorish was where Heaney went to primary school, and Broagh was the location of one of his father's farms; yet both poems have a political perspective that evokes not just idyllic, but contested, landscapes. For example, **'Anahorish'** is 'My "place of clear water"'; Heaney asserts a sense of ownership and identification with this landscape, which is described in pastoral, **prelapsarian** terms.

As in several other poems in *Wintering Out*, water imagery offers a sense of cleansing and renewal: it is the place 'where springs washed into/ the shiny grass/ and darkened cobbles/ in the bed of the lane.' Despite offering such an idyllic view of an ancient world – where, later, 'mound-dwellers' go 'to break the light ice/ at wells' – and indicating that little has changed for centuries, there is a writerly sense about the poem which suggests that although the poet identifies strongly with this place, it is not one to which he fully belongs in the present tense. The poet sees the landscape in linguistic terms, experiencing its innocence through the educated eyes of experience: the name of the place – that is, the proper noun – is what produces the poem as much as the place itself: 'soft gradient/ of consonant, vowel-meadow'. **'Broagh'** uses its harsher sound to make explicit the conflict. The landscape and the place-name merge in an image of a footprint that forms one of the letters of the name:

> The garden mould
> bruised easily, the shower
> gathering in your heelmark
> was the black *O*
>
> in *Broagh*,

The poems and poem commentaries

Note the Edenic imagery, but notice how, this time, it is the imagery not of innocence but of experience. The garden bears signs of bruising, which perhaps has a linguistic echo of God's words of rebuke to Eve in the Garden of Eden, when he told her that the serpent would 'bruise' her head. The 'heelmark' seems to be a stain or a sign of sin, and it gathers sinister-looking black rain. Even the names of natural elements might be taken to have belligerent connotations. The shower makes a sound like military drums – 'its low tattoo' – the rhubarb is sharp and threatening, since it has blades, and perhaps even the 'windy boortrees' carry a sense of being hooligans (boors). The very pronunciation of the place-name enacts a conflict as the poem ends on the ominous note of 'strangers' (a typical word for English invaders in Irish literature) being unable to pronounce the final '*gh*' sound of Broagh. This also carries a sense of rebellion, since finding the name 'difficult to manage' has an analogue in the English invaders finding the native Irish people hard to control.

Irish life is far from idyllic in two disturbing poems in *Wintering Out*, **'Bye-Child'** and **'Limbo'**. Both concern unwanted children – the latter depicting a baby boy thrown into the sea, the former a boy kept in a hen house with minimal sustenance and without any care. Each seems to have roots in reality and both begin with a journalistic element. **'Bye-Child'**, based on the 1956 incident of a seven year-old boy found in County Down, begins with an epigraph – '*He was discovered in the henhouse where she had confined him. He was incapable of saying anything.*' – that sounds like a television or radio report; and the first two lines of 'Limbo' proceed in the manner of a newspaper report offering answers to the Ws of Who, What and When: 'Fishermen at Ballyshannon/ Netted an infant last night'. But the poems are anything but tabloid in style. Rather than sensationalise, they humanise.

In 'Bye-Child' the speaker identifies with the boy who lived among chickens, tenderly referring to him as 'Little moon man' and imagining the sensory experiences of living in the henhouse from his perspective:

> … the dust,
>
> The cobwebs, old droppings
> Under the roosts
> And dry smells from scraps

In **'Limbo'** the speaker identifies with the woman who murdered her child, imagining her to have been 'Ducking him tenderly'.

In these poems there is an absence of blame. Yet perhaps there is a contextual subtext to consider that is hinted at in the poems. The death of the boy in 'Limbo' is called 'An illegitimate spawning' and bye-child is a Victorian term for an illegitimate child, often one born to a servant after a union with the head of the household. So, the poems might be exploring the plight of those at the bottom of the social spectrum and thus implicitly questioning the way that Irish

Taking it further ▶

The Northern Irish playwright Brian Friel also explores issues of colonialism and language in his play *Translations*. See, for example, Act Two, Scene One when Yolland, an English soldier, expresses frustration at his inability to say the word *poteen* (a potato-based spirit pronounced pot-cheen) correctly.

CRITICAL VIEW

According to Michael Parker 'these chilling tales can also be read as parables for the present state of Ireland and its moral paralysis. Tribal taboos and laws can easily outweigh "civilized" humane values' (Parker 1993, p.112). Explain what he means and the extent to which you agree.

NEW SELECTED POEMS 1966–1987

Taking it further ▶

You might want to watch some relatively recent films that explore the repressive nature of Catholic Irish society at times in the twentieth century. For example, *The Magdalen Sisters* (2003), directed by Peter Mullan, deals with the treatment of women who become pregnant out of wedlock.

Context

In Charles Dickens' *Great Expectations*, Miss Havisham is an old woman who still wears her wedding outfit in a room untouched since her wedding day, when she was jilted by her groom.

unheimlich: from German meaning weird, uncanny or unhomely, this term is often used when exploring uncanny effects in literature. See p.12 for further details and a relevant task.

society shuns illegitimacy, with 'Limbo' being a tale of religious exclusion and 'Bye-child' one of social exclusion.

As well as exploring the consequences of unsanctioned sexual encounters in rural Ireland, Heaney is not afraid to turn the spotlight on himself in autobiographical poetry that deals with less than flattering aspects of marriage. **'Wedding Day'** is a brave, self-revealing poem that wrong-foots the reader in its first line. Rather than the hopes and joys that one might expect from the title, he offers a simple three-word statement, 'I was afraid.', whose impact is heightened by it being alone on the line, the shortest in the poem, and the mood, rather than joyful, is gloomy. The speaker replays images of the day and wonders about the 'wild grief' on one man's face and the 'sap/ Of mourning' that was rising in the faces of the wedding guests as the couple prepared to depart in their taxi.

It is difficult to make sense of such feelings without an autobiographical approach. Heaney's sister-in-law, Polly Devlin, in her memoir *All Three of Us*, notes that there is a 'thin membrane … between grief and joy in Irish celebrations' and describes how her sister, Marie Heaney, on her wedding day, gave a 'poignant rendering of the ballad, *Slieve Gallion Brae*', and how Seamus Heaney saw grief on his father-in-law's face (quoted in Parker 1993, p.109). Heaney himself has spoken about the 'moments of strangeness, sudden lancings or fissures in the fun' at a wedding, of which he says 'it is in the literal sense **unheimlich**, an unhoming' (O'Driscoll 2008, p.254). The unnerving sense of the occasion is continued in the poem's penultimate stanza. The young bride is presented in a manner reminiscent of Dickens' Miss Havisham:

> You sing behind the tall cake
> Like a deserted bride
> Who persists, demented,
> And goes through the ritual.

Yet the final stanza might cause us to re-evaluate our response and put the unsettling images down to nervousness and inexperience rather than any incompatibility between husband and wife. The poem climaxes with an image of tenderness which also underlines the speaker's youth and perhaps also shows the new wife taking the place of his mother: 'Let me/ Sleep on your breast to the airport.'

'Summer Home' is another love poem that refuses to romanticise love. Beginning in free verse, the poet addresses a difficulty with his wife directly, using a foul smell as an extended metaphor for something that has soured in the relationship. This is a fitting image: a bad smell can linger and annoy; it suggests something unwell or rotten; it can be troubling and provoke a visceral response, but it can't be seen and its cause is often difficult to identify. The cause of the literal smell is uncovered in the last two-line stanza of the poem's first part — maggots beneath a mat, which the speaker cleans up with boiling water: 'scald, scald, scald'. Perhaps this evokes the hot tears that will be shed during the process of healing which will be difficult and painful. The stanza

The poems and poem commentaries

as a whole might be seen as an introduction to the poem, which not only suggests the problem and the difficulties in identifying it and dealing with it, but also the solution.

Religious imagery and natural imagery suggest a process of healing. The speaker hears his wife's 'small lost weeping' as he gathers wild flowers, which will 'soon taint to a sweet chrism'. Chrism is the oil and balsam used for baptism and other rites in the Catholic Church and, at this point, the final stanza of Section II – given prominence by being a single line with two short sentences both in the imperative voice – the process of healing begins with a religious seriousness: 'Attend. Anoint the wound'. Natural and religious language continues to suggest the healing process in the third section of the poem. The speaker says 'I postulate/ thick healings' – that is, he suggests having sex, with 'postulate' also meaning to seek admission to a religious order, imagery that is carried on in the final line of this section which conveys both a sense of desire and a religious cleansing.

While love is rebuilt slowly and gradually, note how this process is far from smooth and is not without setbacks. The couple 'tented' their wound. I take the verb to suggest covering the wound as one might be covered with a bandage, the tent image being appropriate also to the sheets resembling parts of a tent, and perhaps also carries a religious connotation through the noun 'tent', which is a name for a sweet wine used in Holy Communion.

Yet there is a shift in tone as a more ironic mode is suggested by Heaney's simile describing how the couple 'lay as if the cold flat of a blade/ had winded us'. Read in this way, it seems that rather than having been reconciled through vigorous sex that has left them breathless, the difficulty in the couple's relationship – the nature of it is never spelled out – still leaves them winded. Note how, in the final section, after what we might take to be a sexual union in Section IV, discord resurfaces as the speaker swears at his wife and they lie 'stiff till dawn'.

It is interesting to consider the varied stanzaic forms used by Heaney, and perhaps the last section, with its regular quatrains of iambic pentameter, suggests that the relationship is returning to normal. The final imagery suggests harmony, as the couple, together on an outing to a tourist attraction 'tapped/ Stalactites in the cave's old, dripping dark –/ Our love calls tiny as a tuning fork'. The love is like a force outside of the couple; it seems to call to them. It might make a 'tiny' sound but the aural image, and its role in forming the second part in a poem that rarely contains rhyme suggests that it is clear, harmonious and stable.

The poem might be said to be in keeping with the collection's title. This term 'wintering out' is from farming, and refers to the time when cattle are taken in winter to an area on the farm where they have shelter and are given a minimal diet before being fattened in the spring and summer. The speaker in 'Summer Home' has to winter out a period of hardship before he can progress to happier times.

Enduring hardship is perhaps reflected in poems that deal with more public matters too. It seems that the early 1970s was a difficult time to be endured for

> **TASK**
> Note the different ways in which religious imagery has been used in the poems you have studied so far.

> **TASK**
> Note the various different stanzaic forms that Heaney uses in 'Summer Home'. In what ways might each choice of stanzaic form be related to Heaney's subject matter or to the effects that he is creating? Pay particular attention to times when the stanzaic form shifts within a poem.

NEW SELECTED POEMS 1966–1987

> **Context**
>
> Heaney talks of the picture that inspired the image of the dead men in the farmyards in Section II of 'The Tollund Man'. The picture, from *Guerrilla Days in Ireland* by an IRA commander, Tom Barry, 'was of a farmer's family who had been shot in reprisals … [and] left lying on their backs beside their open door.' (O'Driscoll 2008, p.135)

Heaney's country. **'The Tollund Man'**, for example, meditates on the body of an executed man from the Iron Age to explore aspects of the so-called Troubles in Northern Ireland. The first section of the poem describes, in intricate detail and with hushed reverence, the body of a man exhumed from a Danish bog who has been killed as a sacrifice to a fertility goddess. In the second part, the speaker turns to thoughts of executions in Ireland. He merges Iron Age beliefs with Catholicism, knowing he could 'risk blasphemy' to 'Consecrate the cauldron bog/ Our holy ground and pray' that somehow the sacrificed Danish man might bring new life to men killed in Northern Ireland. A similarity between two types of death is suggested, but the comparison does not establish equivalence: there is perhaps a kind of ritual dignity about a man sacrificed as part of Iron Age religion, but the murder and mutilation of four men – in what we might expect to be a more civilised era – is presented as being much more appalling. A generation of men from one family, it seems, have been executed and their bodies have been trailed along railway lines.

> **Context**
>
> The Northern Ireland Conflict (c1968 -1998) is often known by the euphemistic title 'The Troubles'. It refers to the violence between those in favour of establishing a united Ireland (Nationalists and Republicans who are mostly Catholics) and those in favour of the continued union between Britain and Northern Ireland (Unionists and Loyalists who are mostly Protestants).
>
> More than 3,600 lives were lost.
>
> Some take the conflict as the Civil Rights marches in Derry in 1968, others with the first deployment of British troops to Northern Ireland in 1969.
>
> The end of the conflict is usually taken to be the signing of the Belfast/Good Friday Agreement on 10 April 1998, which set up a power sharing assembly to govern Northern Ireland.
>
> See p.21 for brief definitions of the terms Nationalist, Republican, Unionist and Loyalist.

Taking it further ▶

Heaney's contemporary Derek Mahon, who left Northern Ireland during the Troubles, famously rhymed 'bomb' and 'home' in his poem 'Afterlives'. Compare the presentation of home in Heaney and Mahon. (An internet search should produce a copy of 'Afterlives'.)

Perhaps there is something psychologically unsettling, something – to reapply Heaney's term from his comments on **'Wedding Day'** – *unheimlich* about the feelings engendered by contemplating the bodies from Denmark and Ireland. The poem finishes with the memorable conclusion that

> Out there in Jutland
> In the old man-killing parishes
> I will feel lost,
> Unhappy and at home.

Normally to feel 'at home' means to feel at ease, but the speaker has the uncanny experience where something old, familiar and reassuring – home – has been twisted in its meaning, so rather than comforting, it disturbs.

Heaney explores another aspect of the tensions between communities in Northern Ireland in a more direct, but subtle way in **'The Other Side'**. Here the subject matter is not of life and death, but just how every day interactions are slightly different when dealing with people who have a different religious background. Heaney's poem is based on his family's relationship with a Protestant neighbour. It is a dramatic, narrative poem, with snippets of dialogue that help characterise the neighbour, who seems to view life from an upstanding Protestant, even Puritan, perspective. His 'It's as poor as Lazarus, that ground' sets the tone, and, initially, there is the sense that he is unpleasant and superior: suggesting that the speaker's family's ground is inferior to his, with the 'tongue of the chosen people'. He even makes disparaging comments on the family's religion: 'Your side of the house, I believe,/ hardly rule by the book at all.' The speaker characterises his brain as 'a whitewashed kitchen … swept tidy/ as the body o' the kirk'. Yet, if we look closer, Heaney's depiction may be more balanced. There is something mean-spirited about the way in which his family mocks the neighbour: 'For days we would rehearse/ each patriarchal dictum', and everything about the way the neighbour calls while the speaker's family is at prayer is respectful: it was 'not until after the litany' when he would announce his presence at their door. The poem ends by the perspective shifting more fully towards the speaker and his uncertainty about how to behave towards the neighbour. Note the three half rhymes that slow the movement in the penultimate stanza and the single line stanza that completes its question. There has been a shift from the mocking tone of the second section of the poem to something closer to an understanding of the neighbour and an acknowledgement of social awkwardness on both sides. The extent to which the poem suggests that there might be meaningful or worthwhile relationship between the people in the poem, or, by extension, between the two 'sides' in Northern Ireland is a matter for you to debate.

From *Stations* (1975)

Published as a pamphlet (small book), these prose poems are autobiographical and address experiences from different stages of Heaney's life. **'Nesting-Ground'** explores childhood fears and uncertainty as the speaker thinks about putting his hand deep into a sandmartins' nest, but is fearful as he recalls having been shown a rat's nest in a corn stack. The poem's final image is of a tentative boy who watches and listens, but is too cautious to act. **'Cloistered'** evokes boarding life at a Catholic school, describing the scene as he sits with other students in a study hall. It is all so vivid to him that he could compile a richly illustrated book, detailing the activities of each time of the day. The poem continues, offering sensuous evocations of the cold study hall and the sounds of

> **CRITICAL VIEW**
> Michael Parker suggests that 'one must question the value of a conversation only able to embrace superficial topics such as "the weather" and "the price of grass-seed"' (Parker, 1993, p.103).

> **CRITICAL VIEW**
> Helen Vendler argues that the speaker develops empathy as the poem progresses and that Heaney offers a 'faceted, many-sided portrait' of 'someone outside the poet's ethnic group' (Vendler H., *Seamus Heaney*, Harvard University Press, 2000, p.83).

> **TASK**
> Write about the ways in which Heaney presents the Protestant neighbour in 'The Other Side'. To what extent do you agree that Heaney's depiction is an example 'of a dangerous Catholic stereotyping'? (E. Andrews, *The Poetry of Seamus Heaney*, Columbia University Press, 1998, p.81).

a supervising priest passing as he works on maths or Latin. It concludes with the image of the exhilaration of the young speaker as he breaks ice on his water jug at the start of a new day. 'England's Difficulty', 'Visitant' and 'Trial Runs' offer youthful encounters with the Second World War. **'England's Difficulty'** details the child's experience of being taken, on the shoulders of an adult, to see the Belfast sky during the Blitz. The poem is encircled by the speaker's reflections on his state of being neither on one side of the conflict nor the other: in the first line he is 'a double agent' and in the last sentence, he crosses the lines (presumably of both camps) and reports back to no one (since he has no allegiance to either side). **'Visitant'** recalls the Sunday visit of a German prisoner of war (POW) to his aunt's house. In the central section, he lists the gifts, made in prison, that were given to the families visited. At the beginning and the end of the poem, he is presented as other-worldly (the title means both a visitor and a supernatural being) and there is a sense of the speaker being in both camps as we hear of the 'judgements of captor and harbourer'. **'Trial Runs'** narrates the story of the Protestant neighbour returning from war. He gives the speaker's father rosary beads as a gift and the men joke. Beneath this banter, the speaker feels, is the nervous awareness of their religious and political differences.

'The Stations of the West' narrates the experience of a stay in a Gaeltacht region – a part of Ireland where Irish is the first language. The speaker details the custom of having spit and ash smeared on his lips, but expresses the disappointment of only managing 'a few words' of Irish. In the final paragraph, however, he recalls the mysterious power of the language as he remembers the stations (places of pilgrimage) in impressive, glowing terms. It is not the places, but the names he recalls. He thinks of their holiness and their latent power: 'names portable as altar stones/unleavened elements'. The final poem from *Stations*, **'Incertus'**, looks ahead to Heaney's vocation as a poet. Its title is the pen name under which Heaney's first poems were published and it means unsure or uncertain, showing Heaney's modesty and diffidence. Its final image is of a 'mouldering tegument' – a decaying outer layer that is tough and protective.

Commentary Heaney uses prose poems to evoke epiphanies – moments of heightened experience, when ordinary perceptions are charged with radiance or revelation. The term is associated with the influential Irish writer James Joyce (1882–1941) and his influence is perhaps also present in **'Cloistered'** whose setting resembles early parts of Joyce's autobiographical bildungsroman, *A Portrait of the Artist as a Young Man* (1916) in which Joyce's alter ego, Stephen Dedalus, describes life in a Catholic boarding school in sensuous, naturalistic detail. The seemingly innocent poring over a single word – which is evident at the start of **'England's Difficulty'** is also seen in Joyce's work. For example, in the first paragraph of 'The Sisters', the opening story in *Dubliners* (1914), the boy narrator says the word 'paralysis' to himself. In Heaney's poem, '"enemy" had the toothed efficiency of a/mowing machine'. Note the connotations of both fear and admiration. Despite the gently amused tone of the older speaker at his younger self, the grappling with the word perhaps exemplifies the uncomfortable condition of the Catholic Irish Nationalist regarding the world wars. To some degree, Germany and Britain are both enemies. The speech of the unnamed adult – "When the Germans bombed Belfast it was the/bitterest Orange parts [that is, those loyal to Britain] were hit the worst" – might be taken to show some empathy with the Germans and to suggest their sympathies with the Catholics in Northern Ireland. Yet, as in much of Joyce's prose, there is a sense that an experience has been recorded vividly and objectively; the feelings and opinions of the writer are out of reach. Note that, as often in Northern Ireland, the outward subject matter conceals a deeper concern. The title refers not just to the difficulties caused by being at war with Germany, but the war within Ireland itself. 'England's difficulty is Ireland's opportunity' is an old **Republican** slogan that has been used many times, by, for example, the rebels of Easter 1916 who struck during the middle of the First World War. Despite being surrounded by Republican speech, it would seem that the speaker wants to preserve his neutrality and nowhere does this seem more important than in the realm of language. The lines he crosses are linguistic ones, which he crosses with 'carefully enunciated passwords'.

Speech and the subtext that lies beneath it are also important subjects in **'Trial Runs'**. Note how Heaney uses dialogue like a dramatist to convey characterisation, theme and subject. The poem's conclusion foregrounds the subject of the conversation, suggesting it is a cover for a territorial struggle between Catholic and Protestant, who, despite their outwardly joshing cockiness, are 'two big nervous birds dipping and lifting,/making trial runs over a territory'. Yet this might not be the whole story. As with 'The Other Side' there is a complexity and a sensitivity to Catholic–Protestant relations. The Protestant thinks enough of his Catholic neighbour to bring him back a present and their dialogue forms a genuinely funny exchange of repartee. Both enjoy each other's company and share laughter. The speaker's father begins by wittily using Protestant language, using the word 'papish' (still in use among some Ulster Protestants, but archaic elsewhere) as he ironically suggests he might have been converted. This provokes the ludicrous image of the Protestant neighbour stealing the beads from the pope's dresser. Finally, the speaker's father concludes the exchange with another comic image, but one that perhaps suggests their shared farming heritage: 'You could harness a donkey with them.' The poem's final sentiments about the nervous birds and the disputed territory mark a shift of tone and a more serious theme, which is also suggested in the opening lines, with the graffiti and the banners. It might be the 1940s, but memories of a Protestant victory in the seventeeth century (the Battle of the Boyne, 1690) are still fresh.

From *North* (1975)

North marks a significant development in Heaney's poetry. Its title refers to both the northern lands of the Vikings but also, of course, to the North of Ireland. But before confronting the conflict in poems that are perhaps more direct and arresting than ever, the collection begins with two poems that celebrate a

Nationalists want a united Ireland ruled from Dublin.

Republicans want a united Ireland and support or will accept violence as a means to this end. The vast majority of Nationalists and Republicans are from Catholic backgrounds.

Unionists want to maintain independence from the Republic of Ireland and remain part of the United Kingdom.

Loyalists back the union and support or will accept violence as a means of retaining it. The vast majority of Unionists and Loyalists are from Protestant backgrounds.

simple, wholesome life. **'Sunlight'** focuses on a single subject: Heaney's aunt who lived with the family at their farm called Mossbawn. It begins with images of the yard, then describes typical actions as the aunt bakes. Moving into the present tense, the speaker describes her preparing scones then resting while they rise. The poem concludes with the thought that his aunt's actions are, or she represents, love, which he compares with a homely image from baking: a 'scoop/ sunk past its gleam/ in the meal-bin'.

> ### Context
> Heaney's Aunt Mary was a 'tower of emotional strength, unreflective in a way but undeceived about people or things.' Heaney remembers how 'When the hay was being carried in for the cows, there'd be a little trail of it left between the stack and the byre door. Mary used to milk the cows in that byre and, in my mind, she was the familiar spirit of the hay and the yard'. (O'Driscoll 2008, p.171)

CRITICAL VIEW
Michael Parker writes that 'The poet's earnest prayer is that those in the North who have died in the Troubles may achieve in death the serenity of Gunnar Hamundarson' who 'has earned a respite from the feuding' (Parker 1993, p.132).

TASK
Read the two Critical view features on 'Funeral Rites'. Explain which view comes closer to your own.

'The Seed Cutters' depicts the actions of workers who prepare potato seed for planting. These might have taken place at any time during the last few hundreds of years, and the poet identifies with them, including himself in the picture. Heaney moves from the comforts of the past to the disturbances of the present in **'Funeral Rites'**. The poem is in three sections. It begins with one detailing his experiences of natural deaths in the family, describing the rosary beads wrapped around dead hands, the knuckles, the shroud and the quilted coffin as well as the candles. Nails are hammered into the coffin and it moves on like a 'black glacier'. The second section shifts to the present tense and to the deaths that come in consequence of the Northern Ireland conflict. The speaker expresses the need for comfort and remembrance. 'We pine for ceremony', he says then imagines a dream of restoration for all communities, where the dead could be laid to rest in the megalithic burial mounds of the Boyne valley in the centre of Ireland. Perhaps by going beneath the conflict to a shared, pre-Christian past, healing might be achieved. The final section imagines the people driving away from the burial mound. The speaker thinks of those buried as being of a similar temperament to the tenth-century Viking chieftain, Gunnar Hámundarson, who died in battle. Even though his killing had – thus far – gone unavenged, he was said to have been at peace in his burial chamber, his face looking at the moon with an expression of joy.

CRITICAL VIEW
Heather O'Donoghue views the reference to the Icelandic chieftain as being more complex and troubling: 'Gunnar's joyful expression is not serenity, but the exultancy that he died a hero, and in the confident expectation that he will be avenged' (in Bernard O'Donoghue (ed.), *The Cambridge Companion to Seamus Heaney*, Cambridge: Cambridge University Press, 2009, p.200).

The poems and poem commentaries

The next two poems also use Viking subject matter. **'North'** imagines Viking raids on Ireland, the violence of which suggest continuity with the Northern Irish conflict in the 1970s. The speaker hears the voices of the Viking raiders warning him, and the poem concludes with instructions from the Vikings' longship telling him how he should write poetry. He must trust his own judgement and 'Compose in darkness', be prepared for hard work ('the long foray'), not expect easy torrents of inspiration ('no cascade of light'), and be prepared to use his own lived and felt experience ('trust the feel of what nubbed treasure/ [his] hands have known').

> **CRITICAL VIEW**
>
> Neil Corcoran writes of the quotation at the end of 'North': 'Heaney's fiction of being advised by a Viking voice establishes a frightening intimacy between the sources of his poetry and the brutal facts of Viking culture and power … the poet … is engaged, like the Vikings, on a "foray": a hostile or predatory incursion, a raid' (Neil Corcoran, *The Poetry of Seamus Heaney: A Critical Study*, London: Faber & Faber, 1998, p.57).

> **TASK**
>
> Study the critical view, then discuss your ideas and responses with other members of your class.

'Viking Dublin: Trial Pieces' proceeds by means of association and begins with the speaker contemplating an artefact in a museum: a piece of bone form Viking times. An incision prompts him to wonder if the mark is part of an artwork – a trial piece – drawn on bone. Other exhibits are considered and a magnified drawing is imagined as a Viking longship sailing up Dublin's River Liffey, its hostile intent concealed beneath the coins and bone pins it carried as a currency for trade. The speaker moves from considering the exhibition to his own writing and this identification with Scandinavia brings him to identify with Shakespeare's Danish prince, Hamlet. Heaney is self-lacerating as he mocks his ineffectuality with imagery of 'jumping in graves,/ dithering, blathering'. The Troubles and how to respond to them comes into sharper focus in the poem's penultimate section as the speaker invites his Viking ancestors to consider the violence of present-day Northern Ireland. The 'neighbourly, scoretaking/ killers' recalls phrases from 'Funeral Rites' and there is a sense that nothing has moved on, that violence is cyclical. In the poem's final section, the tone lightens through the direct speech of a comic character from Synge's *The Playboy of the Western World*. He talks of the numerous skulls that exist in Dublin, before the speaker closes the poem with imagery of his own words, which 'lick around' the quays of Dublin and 'go hunting/ lightly as pampooties/ over the skull-capped ground'. Perhaps the juxtaposition of the bizarre and the macabre suggests that his words are unlikely to have any effect in the face of violence that has been seen in Ireland since at least Viking times. The idea of licking and of wearing light shoes from the Aran islands (pampooties) to hunt seems both ineffectual and faintly ridiculous.

> **Context**
>
> A trial piece is a piece of art done to practise a skill or test an idea. It was typically a carving done on wood in ancient times.

NEW SELECTED POEMS 1966–1987

> ### Context
> While going into the Republic of Ireland to bury dead might seem unusual for Protestants in Northern Ireland, who wish to remain separate from the rest of Ireland, the Boyne was the site of a famous Protestant victory, that of William III over James II in 1690. This victory is celebrated every July by Protestants in Northern Ireland and its impact can be felt in poems like 'Trial Runs', in which banners declare 'REMEMBER 1690' (see Contexts, p.85).

A piece of bone sparks the speaker's imagination in **'Bone Dreams'**. In this case it is dug up on Heaney's grazing land, and he imagines throwing it defiantly at England. In his mind, he follows the bone through time as the poem explores the English language, like an archaeologist of words, and how the past is connected to the present. The relationship to England that it depicts is complicated; there is distaste at the linguistic colonisation of Ireland, but a love of English also emerges, expressed through the English landscape.

A much more violent union between the English and Irish landscapes occurs in **'Act of Union'**, whose title refers both to sex and the act of parliament that joined Ireland to England in 1801. The speaker is England who addresses Ireland, the woman he has wronged. The 'heaving province where our past has grown' is both the unborn child of the rape and Northern Ireland. In the poem's second section the speaker turns to consider how this offspring will cause pain for them both: his fists are already beating at her from within and 'they're cocked' at him 'across the water'. It ends with an image of hurt in the future as the woman will be 'raw, like opened ground, again'.

Ideas of conquest are also explored allegorically in **'Hercules and Antaeus'**. In Greek mythology, Antaeus was a giant from Libya who made all passing strangers wrestle with him. As his strength was renewed every time he made contact with the ground, he was invincible. Hercules, however, had the cunning to lift him up and crush him to death. Heaney's Hercules is a coloniser, who, with his 'black powers' and 'intelligence' dispossesses the giant. Antaeus is presented as one of a line of beaten heroes: from Balor, the Celtic King of the Fomorians, to Sitting Bull, the Native American who was killed by General Custer. The poem ends with an image of the defeated giant becoming the landscape, which is offered as 'pap for the dispossessed' – a false hope that at once feeds and deceives the colonised people.

North is well known for its central section of bog poems. Heaney's inspiration for these came largely from his reading of *The Bog People* (1969), an illustrated account by the archaeologist P.V. Glob of the well-preserved Iron Age bodies that were recovered from bogs in Northern Europe. **'Bog Queen'** imagines the decomposition of a female Viking body – this time one found in

The poems and poem commentaries

Northern Ireland, in the estate of Lord Moira in the late eighteenth century. **'The Grauballe Man'** recasts a victim of paramilitary violence as an Iron Age man who was thought to have had his throat slit and been offered up as a sacrifice to a fertility god. **'Strange Fruit'** depicts the beheaded head of a bog woman that stares disconcertingly at the viewer. **'Punishment'** considers the body of what is simultaneously a Iron Age dead woman sacrificed and exhumed from a peat bog and a woman from Northern Ireland who has been tarred and feathered by women in her community as a punishment for a relationship with a British soldier.

Context

In the mid-1970s Heaney's interest in the bog people went beyond Glob's book. The poet Ted Hughes encouraged Heaney to write more bog poems, and, in October 1973, he went at the invitation of the Danish Association of English Teachers to Denmark, where he saw the Tollund Man and the Grauballe Man.

▲ The Grauballe Man, preserved remains of human from 1st century BC, Moesgard Museum, Denmark

The second half of *North* considers aspects of the Northern Irish conflict more directly and in less condensed language. **From 'Whatever You Say Say Nothing'** gives voice to some of the clichés and the inadequate nature of language used in Northern Ireland and **from 'Singing School'** offers autobiographical experiences that mostly explore aspects of sectarianism and the conflict, but also his poetic development and his responsibilities as a writer.

Commentary 'Mossbawn: Two Poems in Dedication' are tender poems concerned with a simple, wholesome, almost prelapsarian, life. They are dedicated to Heaney's aunt, Mary. The descriptions in the first, **'Sunlight'**, have been compared to the paintings of Vermeer and have sensuous qualities of light, water and heat: the 'sunlit absence' as the aunt leaves the yard to go into the kitchen, the heat of the iron of the pump, the 'honeyed' water and the sun 'like a griddle cooling' render a simple farmyard scene precious, pleasurable and beautiful. It is a self-effacing poem; there is no single use of the first person pronoun. All of the focus is upon the scene and his aunt's place within that scene, and the central action – the wholesome and generous act of baking – is reminiscent of the poems of simple country crafts that we read of in the poet's early collections. But here there is no sense of cruel nature or burgeoning adolescence and its associated loss of innocence. Instead of climaxing with a realisation of dangers or a sense of fear, the overwhelming feelings of security and contentment felt by the speaker in his childhood are palpable throughout the poem. It achieves this through the homely image of 'a tinsmith's scoop/ sunk past its gleam/ in the meal-bin' – which is a simile for love. The gleaming light of the poem's final image links his aunt with the glowing of luxurious sunshine at the start of the poem and in the title.

After the second poem in dedication, **'The Seed Cutters'**, and its cry out for a world, inspired by the Flemish Renaissance artist Breughel and Irish farming of the traditional staple, potatoes, we move to a much darker place. Here, rather than reading of the passing by natural causes of a loved one expressed in gentle celebratory verse, we are confronted abruptly with deaths of a different sort: the 'neighbourly' murders of the Troubles. Though *North* starts with an outbreak of sunshine, its prevailing mood is bleak. This is obvious, not only in the poems that draw on the savagery from earlier eras, but also in poems that evoke what in Northern Ireland in the 1970s passed for normal life. For example, it might be said that there is a hardening in Heaney's depictions of cross-community relationships. While there are even-handed representations of Catholic–Protestant relationships in earlier collections – in poems such as 'The Other Side', 'Visitant', 'England's Difficulty' and 'Trial Runs' – those in *North* lack the humour and overtures of friendship seen in earlier work. Instead they are marked by fear and mistrust. Such relationships are also more polarised, and they often are between Catholics and the police. **'The Ministry of Fear'** has a sense of the rude intrusion of the political into private life as the young speaker, fresh from a nervy courtship (in which his 'fingers [were] tight as ivy' on the shoulders of the young woman he was kissing goodnight), encounters the unwanted attentions of the police. The strangeness and abruptness of this intrusion are reflected by the sudden shift mid-sentence from pleasing pastoral images – 'the air/ All moonlight and a scent of hay' – to 'policemen/ Swung their crimson flashlamps'. Their presence is rendered by an uncanny image of them being 'black cattle' who crowd around his car. Aggressive, phallic imagery follows as the 'muzzle of a sten-gun' is pointed in the speaker's eye as he is questioned. The italicised '*Seamus?*' suggests a prejudiced attitude: since his name indicates he is a Catholic, he is treated with suspicion.

The same sense of people in Northern Ireland jumping to prejudiced conclusions is evoked in ***from* 'Whatever You Say Say Nothing'**, when the poet's Christian name is characterised as being 'sure-fire Pape'. Heaney's choice of words is interesting: although expressed comically, the line including 'sure-fire'

The poems and poem commentaries

suggests the attitude of those who would shoot a person simply for being a Catholic. It seems people in Northern Ireland size one another up and make snap judgements on religion; their minds are 'as open as a trap'.

Heaney wrote that after the onset of the Troubles, his poetry 'moved from being simply a matter of achieving the satisfactory verbal icon to being a search for images and symbols adequate to our predicament' (Heaney 1984, p.56). Many see this search being realised in the bog poems of *Wintering Out* and *North*.

'Bog Queen' is a dramatic monologue, in which the bog queen describes the effects of time and the bog on her body. She is presented, not rotting, but interacting with the landscape and waiting. Towards the end of the poem, she describes how parts of her have been taken by those who have discovered her: first 'the wet nest' of her hair; then, after he had initially laid her back to rest, a turfcutter took a plait. In the last stanza, she describes how she 'rose' again, and her rising seems more like a resurrection than a discovery. The poem might be considered in the aisling tradition of Irish poetry – the genre in which a dream vision personifies Ireland in the form of a woman. In this case, the poem offers a vision of Ireland as a dignified queen, who while cast down and dormant is resilient and will rise to her glory once more.

'The Grauballe Man' is written in the third person. The first six quatrains describe the body in natural terms: aspects such a river (the tar-like bog in which he lies), a tree (his wrists have a grain like that of a bog oak) and a range of water creatures (such as his instep which is 'cold as a swan's foot', his hips which are like the 'ridge/ and purse of a mussel' and his spine like an eel) suggest his integration with the natural world. Such descriptions elevate the bog body to the level of art and something much more significant than the corpse of an anonymous Iron Age peasant. This is made plain in the seventh stanza in which the speaker questions the reader directly: 'Who will say "corpse"/ to his vivid cast?' Note also how the poem's descriptions build to the one of the body's 'slashed throat'. More than being a poetic rendering of a museum exhibit, the poem implicitly asks questions about the relationship between art and violence. A reader might feel troubled by the beautiful way in which the evidence of the murder has been presented, and something even more troubling occurs in the poem's final stanzas. We move away from the poetic immersion in the world of the Iron Age man to the present and a self-reflexive world where the speaker enters the poem and the broader significance of the experience is considered. The relationship between art and violence – 'beauty and atrocity' – is mentioned directly as the speaker recalls seeing a photograph of the Grauballe Man, and the poem closes with a chain of associated images. The first is of the Dying Gaul – a beautiful marble statue of a Celt who has been fatally wounded by a conquering Roman – and the last of people who have died as a result of

Taking it further

Edna Longley argues that Heaney 'excludes the intersectarian issue, warfare *between* tribes, by concentrating on the Catholic psyche as bound to immolation [sacrifice], and within that immolation to savage tribal loyalties' (Longley 1996, p.154). In your own words, explain what she means, and by making close reference to examples from *North* explore the extent to which you agree.

CRITICAL VIEW

Helen Vendler offers the following high praise for the collection: 'there is no other body of work about those years [1968–1975] that so wholly evokes the desperation and devastation felt in that period … That so many readers, both in Ireland and abroad, have found *North* an unforgettable book means that Heaney's archaeologies have consolidated the personal into the communicable' (Vendler 2000, p.55).

TASK

Choose one of the critical views on *North*. Explain the extent to which you agree, using close references to the poems.

---

sectarian violence in contemporary Northern Ireland: 'each hooded victim,/ slashed and dumped'.

Of those poems, the most controversial is **'Punishment'**. Most responses from within Northern Ireland to this poem (and to those in *North* that deal with the conflict) were critical. For example, former IRA member, Eoghan Harris, wrote that we have nothing to learn from Heaney's poetry, 'it deals with pre-Christian people who put bodies in Danish bogs, not post-Christian people who put them in binliners Its literally bogged down in the past' ('The Glittering Prize' in *Fortnight,* November 1995, p.6). Many seized on the details of 'Punishment', in particular its last lines, and were quick to censure the poet. Ciaran Carson reads the speaker's understanding of the situation as offensive: he thinks it is 'almost as a consolation' and he goes on to remark that it is as if Heaney 'is saying, suffering like this is natural; these things have always happened, they happen now, and that is sufficient ground for understanding and absolution' (Ciaran Carson, *The Honest Ulsterman*, 50 (Winter 1975), p.184). Edna Longley questions the speaker's ambiguous response, which simultaneously empathises with both the feelings of the victim and the perpetrators: 'can the poet run with the hare ("I can feel the tug/ of the halter") and hunt with the hounds?' (Edna Longley, *Poetry in the Wars*, Bloodaxe: Newcastle upon Tyne, 1996, p.154).

Yet it is also possible to respond sympathetically. It might be argued that there is real bravery to the way in which Heaney explores the feelings that a Catholic might have when probing deeply into their response to an act of violence – in this case it is the tarring and feathering of a Catholic woman in revenge for her relationship with a British soldier. The understanding that Heaney's speaker extends is not quite to a paramilitary act of bombing or shooting, but to the maintenance of a kind of tribal solidarity by means of an act of public humiliation. It is, of course, difficult to separate the strands of Heaney's narrative, and the sense of the Iron Age blending into the 1970s clouds and colours the reader's response. But, perhaps one type of punishment that the critics ignore is the self-punishment of the speaker. By laying bare his worst feelings (which are nearly always taken by critics to be the unmediated thoughts and feelings of Heaney) – that he understands 'the exact/ and tribal, intimate revenge', he leaves himself exposed to attack from all sides. The poem is a kind of *exposure* and the dangers of such a strategy are clear from the collection's last poem which bears that name. Here there is a sense of a poet going very much his own way, enduring people talking about him behind his back, feeling the hard enmity of others and even being unable to rely on the advice of friends. What Heaney does in 'Punishment' is, however, the reverse of the norm: he refuses to subscribe to the platitudes such as those detailed in *from* 'Whatever You Say Say Nothing' like 'Oh, it's disgraceful' and 'Where's it going to end?'.

The poems and poem commentaries

> **CRITICAL VIEW**
>
> The poet Ciaran Carson wrote in a review of *North* that 'Heaney seems to have moved – unwillingly, perhaps – from being a writer with the gift of precision, to become a laureate of violence – a mythmaker, an anthropologist of ritual killing, an apologist for "the situation", in the last resort, a mystifier' (Ciaran Carson, quoted in Andrews, 1998, pp.84–5).

From **'Whatever You Say Say Nothing'** contrasts with the dense language and layered allusiveness of the bog poems, offering a conversational commentary on some of the ways in which the conflict in Northern Ireland is discussed and represented. The first four quatrains take a dim view of journalism: the words of the reporter who seeks 'views/ On the Irish thing' sound both euphemistic, inadequate and intrusive, and the way in which the press men 'sniff and point' almost literalises the term 'newshound'. The journalistic clichés, such as 'crack down', 'provisional wing' and 'long-standing hate' and the efforts of both journalists and politicians ('Who've scribbled down' their accounts of the events of the conflict) are both satirised by Heaney.

The ways in which people talk about events are also useless. Heaney quotes empty phrases and the implication is that everyone has something to say about the Troubles, but – to paraphrase the poem's title – what they actually say is nothing. The other meaning of the title – counselling reserve and repression is explored in Section III: the 'famous/ Northern reticence', the idea that 'Religion's never mentioned here' and 'the tight gag of place/ And times'. Language is to be used cautiously and is potentially incendiary: 'tongues lie coiled, as under flames lie wicks'.

The final quatrain in Section III presents the Troubles as a siege within a siege: the Catholics are confined in Northern Ireland, like the Greeks in the wooden horse in Troy. Although a comical image, perhaps the implication is that they will break out heroically and end up victorious over their oppressors. Black humour continues in Section IV with the quoting of the graffiti in Ballymurphy which reads 'Is there a life before death?' Ballymurphy is the area of Belfast where eleven Catholic men had been shot dead in August 1971 by British paratroopers who had been sent to intern suspected IRA terrorists. With grim comedy, the graffiti reverses the question 'is there life after death?', perhaps suggesting that, for some in Northern Ireland, existence barely constitutes life. Yet beneath the humour of the poem lies a grim endurance and despair: 'We hug our little destiny again'.

From **'Singing School'** has six parts, which detail autobiographical instances of Northern Irish life during the Troubles of the 1970s. **'1 The Ministry of Fear'** is dedicated '*For Seamus Deane*' and is written as a verse letter to his friend, who attended the same school, St Columb's College, Derry. Heaney, who boarded, recalls various experiences, such as extreme homesickness, exchanging poems with Deane, the corporal punishment meted out by the

> **CRITICAL VIEW**
>
> Edna Longley writes of the final stanza of 'The Ministry of Fear' that Heaney suggests all poets from the North of Ireland are, like Yeats, motivated 'by a desire to show English poets that they can make better use of [their] lyric inheritance' (Edna Longley, *The Living Stream*, Newcastle upon Tyne: Bloodaxe, 1994, p.200).

NEW SELECTED POEMS 1966–1987

> **CRITICAL VIEW**
>
> *I was in a hotel up around County Monaghan one night, feeling strange and poetically barren, and there was a dance on, a lot of country kids listening to pop music, and about half past one they came out over the car park, and these absolute dialect voices came bubbling up to me. It was like a vision of the kind of life I had in the fifties, going to dances and so on, and I felt the redemptive quality of the dialect, of the guttural, the illiterate self.*
>
> (Seamus Heaney quoted in John Haffenden *Seamus Heaney Viewpoints: Poets in Conversation*, London: Faber & Faber, 1981. pp.57–58)

Context

Hedge-schools were first set up after the suppression of Catholic education, first under Oliver Cromwell in the 1650s and then under the Penal Laws (sets of laws passed by England in Ireland to curb the powers of Catholics).

In the first of the **'Glanmore Sonnets'**, rural and creative growth and fertility go hand in hand and the octave culminates with the thoughts: 'art a paradigm of earth new from the lathe/ Of ploughs. My lea is deeply tilled.' The speaker is inspired by his surroundings, but the sestet ends with tension. After a long pause marked by ellipsis, ghosts disrupt the mood of contentedness and plenty – these ghosts are possibly distractions, old ways of working that he thought he'd escaped or troubling memories of the past. The sense of the power of these ghosts to disturb is reinforced by rhyme: the optimism of the farmland, which is like 'a dark unblown rose' rhymes with the ghosts, which are like 'freakish Easter snows'.

In Sonnet II, at the centre of the octave is a quotation from a sculptor friend of Heaney's from Belfast: 'These things are not secrets but mysteries'. The speaker, in Glanmore, takes comfort from not having to rationalise, but to learn from his environment. He likens it to a 'hedge-school' – a type of informal school that was set up, often outdoors under the shelter of a hedge or farm building. Like the Romantic poets, Heaney recognises the educative powers of nature and the need to experience, rather than to learn everything through study, but the reference also has a political overtone.

There is a sense of liberation, as Heaney escapes the structures and the political unrest in the North and reconnects to a more rural Ireland that is not only far away from the British province of Northern Ireland but far from the city life of Dublin. It is in this place of freedom, which is more like the landscape of his rural Derry childhood, that he is able to find his poetic voice with ease. Interestingly the subject matter of his poem – as it is for many in *Field Work* – is not a memory of childhood or some distant event, or a reflection recast through Iron Age history, but the more immediate experience of living in the present in Glanmore. Note the rhythms of Irish speech as 'Vowels ploughed into other' and the joy of the poetic creation, which comes as naturally as ploughed ground in a fertile field: 'opened ground,/ Each verse returning like the plough turned round.'

The third sonnet expresses joy in nature and creativity. There is a sense of happy excess: hearing both cuckoo and corncrake at twilight is 'So much, too much'

The poems and poem commentaries

and the Romantic dimension suggested in earlier sonnets is stated overtly as the speaker refers to himself and his wife as William and Dorothy Wordsworth. The very rustling of the trees is reminiscent of the 'cadences' of poetry. Romanticism continues in the next two sonnets as Heaney makes use of childhood memories. In Sonnet IV, the speaker remembers trying unsuccessfully to hear the noise of an approaching train by placing his ear to the railway line. He does, however, hear a horse responding to the train in another field and the poem concludes with the image of ripples shaking across the drinking water at his farm caused by the vibrations of the train.

Sonnet V centres on a tree and evokes the complexity of both landscape and language. The identity of the tree in question shifted from being a 'bower' – a pleasant shady place – when he and his companions were children, to, later, when they climbed it to being 'a greenish, dank/ And snapping memory' and, later still, in adolescence, the site where their first experimental kisses – '"touching tongues"' – took place. The linguistic complexity centres around the Irish and English names for the tree: the Ulster-Scots dialect word 'boortree', which derives from the Scots pronunciation of bower tree and the English elder or elderberry tree, which has Anglo-Saxon roots. In some ways the poem might be thought to blend Heaney's English poetic heritage and his lived Irish experience. It culminates with imagery that combines both the linguistic and the natural, with this 'etymologist of roots and graftings' falling back in his mind's eye to the tree, now a 'tree-house' – a place to dwell in – if only for a short time where he 'would crouch/ Where small buds shoot and flourish in the hush.'

Sonnet VI narrates the story of a man who cycled across the frozen River Moyola in 1947. His story of daring excites the speaker and his family as they sit in their cottage among snowdrifts in winter. The weather is also important in Sonnet VII as the speaker listens to the radio and imagines the conditions in the places mentioned on the shipping forecast.

A weather feature opens Sonnet VIII, though this time it is lightning and rain, which strike genuine fear into the speaker. The mood is foreboding and anxious. He remembers seeing a magpie inspect a sleeping horse, perhaps seeing if it is dead and therefore food for scavenging, which summons up thoughts of a medieval battlefield. This brings on barely specified fears of what the speaker might meet on the road. The term 'blood-boltered' recalls the ghost of Banquo, the friend that Macbeth had murdered in Shakespeare's play, and the allusion evokes an irrational frightened and guilty state of mind. Indeed, the sonnet is marked by its nervous questions. As well as the fears of what he might meet on the road, he wonders how deep in the woodpile lurks a toad and what welters (possibly, is lying soaked in blood) 'on the crops'.

Arising from these thoughts comes a direct address to the poet's wife. He asks her if she remembers seeing an old woman repeatedly rocking and singing to a baby with Down's Syndrome. Perhaps this remembered image sparks thoughts of human suffering or of maternal comfort including the consolation of song.

Context

Macbeth murdered Banquo in an attempt to prevent the prophesy coming true that Banquo's children would be kings. When Macbeth goes to the witches, they show him a vision of eight kings followed by Banquo's Ghost. He cries out:

> Now I see 'tis true,
>
> For the blood-bolt-ered Ban-quo smiles upon me,
>
> And points to them for his.

William Shakespeare, Macbeth, Act 4, Scene 1

CRITICAL VIEW

Harold Bloom says of Heaney's time in Glanmore, County Wicklow that it 'provoked a renewed understanding that beauty and calm can coexist with darkness and fragility, that the private can never be separate from the public, and that the natural world and man's created world or art/poetry are enmeshed' (Harold Bloom (ed.), *Seamus Heaney: Bloom's Major Poets*, Broomall, PA: Chelsea House, 2003, p.49).

Whatever is the case, the emotionally charged experience leaves him 'upstairs shaking'. As well as comfort, his emotional state has sparked a sexual need. The metaphor of 'birchwood in lightning' could refer simultaneously to his fragile state of mind, or the comfort and fiery sex that he hopes he and his wife will soon enjoy.

In Sonnet IX the wife is the one who is in need of protection. She alerts the speaker to a rat swaying on a tree outside. She wants him to kill it and this intrusion into the life of the mind raises the question: 'Did we come to the wilderness for this?' The vermin summons painful memories of his rural childhood of dead rats speared on pitch-forks at threshing. The rat has gone when he comes out and the poem ends on a foreboding note: his wife's 'face/ Haunts like a new moon glimpsed through tangled glass'. As well as conveying the pallor of her face through fear, the simile alludes to the superstition that to view the moon through glass is bad luck.

The final sonnet closes the sequence on a more pastoral and optimistic note. The speaker imagines himself and his wife sleep on moss in Donegal. First, he thinks of them as Lorenzo and Jessica. (Jessica is the only daughter of Shylock, the Jewish merchant in *The Merchant of Venice*, and Lorenzo is the Christian who elopes with her.) Then he likens them to Diarmuid and Grainne, two great lovers from Irish mythology, who eloped and consummated their love before Diarmuid was killed. The speaker imagines he and his wife being laid out and resembling 'breathing effigies on a raised ground'. Finally, within the dream comes another dream. Alluding to Sir Thomas Wyatt's poem 'They Flee from Me', the speaker recalls the time he and his wife consummated their love, with his wife being cast in the role of the knowing female who says 'how like you this?' to her lover. Her kiss is 'deliberate' and it raises them to 'painful/ Covenants of flesh' and brings 'respite' into their 'dewy dreaming faces'.

'from *Field Work*', as its title suggests, explores experiences from the countryside. III offers vivid descriptions of plants, culminating in a vision of a sunflower and I and IV both evoke the speaker's experiences of being with a woman (presumably his wife) in the fields. In both poems, she blends into the environment and is both everyday and extraordinary. In I, the speaker sees a blackbird's 'perfect eye' watching, before he, in turn, watches the addressee and notices the ordinary detail of her 'vaccination mark/ stretched on [her] upper arm'. In IV, he presses a 'flowering currant' to the back of her hand, which looks like a 'birthmark' on her hand. Perhaps this fits with the sense of rebirth that the Heaneys were said to feel when they moved to Glanmore and the mark in some ways resembles the 'Ordinary, mysterious' quality that was celebrated in 'The Skunk', for here the female is paradoxical as she is 'stained, stained/ to perfection.'

'from *Field Work*', is noteworthy for its poems that explore married love. The poet himself has explained that when he moved to Glanmore he and his wife felt like they were starting anew and that the experience brought them closer.

The poems and poem commentaries

In an interview, Heaney compares the move to the renewal of baptismal vows that was made on the last evening of a spiritual retreat (a period of seclusion for prayer and meditation): 'I'd say that the move we made required something similar, a renewed espousal' (O'Driscoll 2008, p.207). There is a playful and amusing quality about the presentation of the wife in **'An Afterwards'** as she undermines the spiritual qualities of poets in favour of presenting their 'backbiting' and 'egotistical' qualities. In the second stanza, classical and down-to-earth language mix as she lets out an angry stream of adjectives criticising the poets, which culminates in a grisly simile taken from Dante: comparing the poets' behaviour to that of the corrupt nobleman Ugolino, who in Dante's *Inferno* is seen eating the back of the head of another sinner, Archbishop Roger, like a dog gnawing at a bone.

The fantastic scene continues with the wife being helped by Virgil's wife (presumably another long-suffering spouse), while the speaker defends himself, asking 'who wears the bays' (that is, has been crowned with bay laurel leaves, which signify poetic honours) and whose is the life 'Most dedicated and exemplary'. Yet the poem's tone shifts at this point: the hyperbolic language and fantastic situations fade. The poet has neglected his wife and family to pursue his art; could he not have 'Unclenched' and come from his room and have gone out walking with his wife and children 'oftener'? Reaching a climax of emotion expressed in the form of realistic complaint, the sincerity and down-to-earth language of the wife's question contrasts with the speaker's previous one about his poetic laurels and his exemplary life.

The truth expressed in the wife's question hurts the speaker. His guilt is felt sharply, as though he is being gaffed in the neck (a gaff is a barbed stick, used for landing big fish), but then the mood shifts once more and the poem almost ends on a harmonious note. The wife speaks with what might be warmth and understanding: '"You weren't the worst. You aspired to a kind,/ Indifferent, faults-on-both-sides tact."' Yet her words could also be interpreted as subtle criticism – his aspiration might seem limited – and she has the last word in the poem, stating the fact of her husband's neglect: '"You left us first, and then those books, behind."'

More overt love between husband and wife is depicted in two poems that use unlikely animals as vehicles to portray sexual feelings: **'The Otter'** and **'The Skunk'**. The former conveys the weather and mood as the speaker relaxes by a Tuscan poolside, admiring his wife as she swims. At the heart of it, is the speaker's gratitude for his wife and their relationship: in the fourth quatrain of a seven-stanza poem he thanks God and declares that when he holds his wife they 'are close and deep/ As the atmosphere on water.' He suggests their shared past by terming her his 'Otter of memory', and he punningly suggests her vital presence in the present moment by saying she exists in 'the pool of the moment'. The present continuous tense ('Turning', 'Heaving') is used as the speaker delights in watching his wife swim and emerge from the water 'Heavy

NEW SELECTED POEMS 1966–1987

> **CRITICAL VIEW**
>
> Bernard O'Donoghue argues that *Station Island* is 'deeply concerned with issues of public answerability and guilt' (O'Donoghue 2009, p.6). By referring to specific poems, explain the extent to which you agree.

Section VI continues the idea of seeking women on another level in three sonnets. Memories of early sexual feelings spring up as the speaker participates in the religious devotions of the central part of the pilgrimage, the night vigil at St Patrick's Basilica. He remembers a girl he whispered to while playing 'secrets', and feelings of shame surface: '*Don't tell. Don't tell*'. As he leaves the church he feels 'an old pang', remembering his 'long virgin/ Fasts and thirsts' of sexual longing. In the last sonnet, another, more satisfying, sexual experience takes shape as he recalls seeing a young woman's 'honey-skinned/ Shoulder-blades' and experience of being 'Translated, given, under the oak tree.' This is juxtaposed with a five-line translation from Dante, which expresses the poet's gratitude after the intervention of his loved one, Beatrice, has freed him from a dark wood.

The mood changes in **Section VII** when the ghost of a murdered friend recounts the events leading up to his death. The speaker asks forgiveness for his 'timid circumspect involvement'. His friend suggests he has nothing to forgive and disappears. As the speaker reaches the ancient stones of St Brigid's Bed in Section VIII, another ghost greets him: Tom Delaney, an archaeologist who died young. The speaker explains the guilt and emptiness he felt when he visited him for the last time; his friend responds that his anxieties over his impending death had been numbed by working with stone from digs. He also acknowledges that he would have liked to have seen the speaker more frequently and contrasts the fate of the two friends: one the 'lucky poet' and the other who failed to get what 'seemed deserved and promised'.

> **Context**
>
> The ghost in Section VII is based on Tom Delaney, who died of a heart complaint in 1979 at the age of 32. He was the head of the Department of Medieval Archaeology at Queen's University, Belfast.

> **Context**
>
> The murdered man is based on William Strathearn, a friend of Heaney, who was the manager of a village shop and had seven children. Born near Heaney, he had played Gaelic football for Derry County. His killers were two Loyalists and two off-duty policemen.

Speechless, the poet recalls a present Tom gave him of a cast of an abbess from stone carvings made by a talented thirteenth-century mason known as the Gowran master. But before he can look at Tom once more, he has been replaced by Heaney's second cousin, Colum McCartney, who was murdered in a random sectarian attack and about whom Heaney wrote 'The Strand at Lough Beg'. McCartney challenges the speaker for not attending his funeral. Despite the speaker's pleas, the murdered man turns on him, saying he 'confused evasion and artistic tact'. He accuses not only the Protestant who shot him, but also, indirectly, the speaker, suggesting that he is on the pilgrimage as an act of atonement and saying he 'saccharined [his] death with morning dew'.

In Section IX a hunger striker speaks, describing his thoughts and feelings around the time of his death as well as some memories of his terrorist activities.

The speaker feels self-disgust and cries out: 'I repent/ My unweaned life that kept me competent/ To sleepwalk with connivance and mistrust.' He declares that he hates aspects of his very identity, including where he was born, and his biddable, unforthcoming nature.

> **Context**
>
> The man in Section IX is based on Francis Hughes, who came from Bellaghy, the same village as Heaney. He was imprisoned for killing one soldier and wounding another, and for his part in a series of gun and bomb attacks during a six-year period. In prison he joined the hunger strike and died on 12 May 1981. He was the second hunger striker to die. After his death riots broke out in many Nationalist areas of Northern Ireland.

In **Section X**, the thud of earthenware as pilgrims stir in the hostel evokes memories of a mug from the speaker's childhood that was once used as a prop in a play. Now taking a warmer view of his background and recovering from the low point of the previous section, the speaker reaches the end of the poem with dazzling light imagery as the 'sun-filled door' is so bright that 'it could put out fire'.

In **Section XI**, the face of a monk from the speaker's past surfaces and gives him a penance, not in the form of prayer, but through poetry. He must translate a poem by Juan de la Cruz, and this translation makes up the rest of the section.

In the final part of the poem, Section XII, the speaker meets James Joyce, the Irish writer who left Ireland for Europe largely to avoid the pressures of its religion, politics and society. His advice is straightforward and direct. The speaker must 'Cultivate a work lust', avoid being so earnest and strike his own note. He tells the speaker that 'The English language/ belongs to us' and to be individualistic in his writing.

The final sequence of *Station Island*, **'Sweeney Redivivus'**, benefits from confidence won through the soul-searching of the central pilgrimage sequence. The persona is presented as making a virtue out of necessity: he is not so much outcast as liberated, his bird-like state gives him an appreciation of nature and a wide perspective. For example, where he roosts in **'In the Beech'** is a 'tree of knowledge and a 'listening post', and **'The First Flight'** celebrates his exile – away from being 'mired in attachment' and able to master new ways to fly and reach 'the top of [his] bent'. As with the sequence as a whole, the character whose name rhymes with that of the poet might be thought of as his alter ego. Heaney moved away from the North, where some of the harsh criticism – particularly of *North* – stung him and he found new ways to write and new heights of poetic achievement away from any poetic group or movement in the South. Some of the poems are forthright in their censure: **'The Scribes'**

Themes

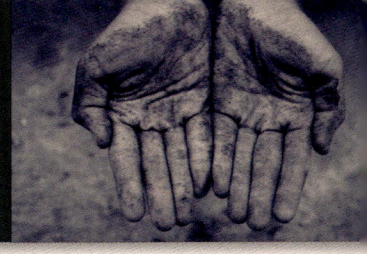

Target your thinking

- What subjects or issues do the poems address; what ideas do they raise or explore? (**AO1**)
- How might your appreciation of the poems' themes and concerns be shaped by your understanding of contexts? (**AO3**)
- If relevant to your exam board, which themes do the Heaney poems and your comparative text share? In what ways might you make thematic connections? (**AO4**)
- In what ways might understanding more about themes open up alternative interpretations of the poems? (**AO5**)

Themes are usually the major ideas or concerns in the text: the topics or issues that the writer wants to explore. Thinking in terms of themes is a useful way to group your thoughts, and you may wish to subdivide a large theme into smaller sub-groups. A literary text, however, is not a simple, unilateral form of communication that seeks to transmit a straightforward message; readers, reviewers and critics often disagree on exactly what constitutes a text's main concerns. Even an author's views on this may not be fixed. Accordingly, themes are not discrete aspects, but are often connected; and part of Heaney's skill is that he often explores several interlinked themes simultaneously.

Throughout your study of *New Selected Poems*, be flexible enough to consider themes in different ways. Your secondary reading, for example, might lead you to consider a new theme or a theme in a new way. If you are studying the text for AQA or WJEC, your study of your comparative text may also help you to see the issues of the poems in a new light. Concentrating on themes that recur in both texts is also a good strategy for study. So, be willing to engage with new themes and new slants on themes you have already considered. This approach will serve you well as a preparation for the examination. After all, the question that you answer might specify an issue or concern of the poetry that you have not considered, or have not considered in this way, before.

Family

When he died in 2013, Heaney was buried in Bellaghy, County Derry, in the same soil his father dug into with his spade and the same soil about which Heaney later wrote. Family and tradition are prevailing concerns, from the poem Heaney recognised as his first, 'Digging', to 'Clearances', the emotional sonnet sequence celebrating his mother. What is remarkable about these poems is their range: from the stunned partial understanding communicated through the third-person narration of 'Mid-Term Break' to the mystical presentation of the quiet father in 'The Stone Verdict'. As well as evoking warm feelings, Heaney's verse gives voice to uncomfortable emotions, such as the frustrations of dealing with an ageing father ('Follower') or the bitterness of marital discord ('The Summer Home').

Heaney also responds to lives of the women, showing both admiration for their lives and work, and an acknowledgement of their struggles. Note, for example, the sense of sheer love in 'Sunlight' in which the speaker describes 'the scone rising/ to the tick of two clocks' – the two clocks symbolise his mother and his aunt – or the homely evocations of folding sheets with his mother in 'Clearances' 5 and the closeness as the pair peel potatoes in 'Clearances' 3. Yet also consider occasions such as the action of ironing in '*Old Smoothing Iron*' which evoke routine hard domestic work and 'the resentment of women'.

Conflict

Since at least the late 1960s, poets in Northern Ireland have faced a tough choice: write about the conflict and be accused of exploiting violence, or don't write about it and be condemned for a lack of social responsibility. Heaney has been impaled on both horns of this dilemma. On one occasion, he was approached by a spokesperson from Sinn Fein (the political wing of the IRA) and asked to write something for the Republican prisoners. While Heaney sympathised with the prisoners, he baulked at being commanded. As he wrote a decade later: 'If I do write something,/ Whatever it is, I'll be writing for myself' ('The Flight Path').

He also was attacked by those who felt his work, particularly *North*, misappropriates violence. Yet many of his poems address the conflict in subtle and sensitive ways – ways that contain indirect political comment, but which also remain true to his poetic ideals. For example, 'Sandstone Keepsake' and 'Chekhov in Sakhalin' respond to the plight of the Republican prisoners. The former comments on the surveillance of the British state and the poet's perceived inadequacies; he is presented as someone 'not worth bothering about'. The latter considers the importance of artistic truth and achieving the right tone – 'not tract' (propaganda) and 'not thesis' (distant academic writing). Even when addressing Republicanism more directly, Heaney is often metaphorical and seems more concerned to explore attitudes than to hammer home a message. He is also able to see people and situations both from the outside and from within. In 'Badgers', for example, he is even–handed: while suggesting that some Catholics admit to feeling 'vaguely honoured' by the actions of the IRA, they are presented ambiguously. One dead badger/IRA man is a 'violent shattered boy', and there is room for the reader to see him as both brave and misguided – one who was possibly manipulated by his elders and superiors in the organisation to carry out his dangerous nocturnal work. Importantly, while Heaney writes from the third-person perspective and is outside of the world of the IRA man, he recognises that, had circumstances been otherwise, he might have been in his position. This is

Taking it further ▶
Read 'The Flight Path' and find out more about the incident that inspired it, which was widely reported in the newspapers. The poem is included in the 1996 collection, *The Spirit Level*.

in 'The Guttural Muse' and a mysterious woman in 'A Dream of Jealousy'. There are also more unusual takes on the love poem: 'Act of Union' refers to both an act of parliament and a sexual act; 'Punishment' deals with the consequences of a forbidden sexual relationship and features a speaker who is half in love with the victim (the Catholic woman who was tarred and feathered).

Faith

In many of the poems, Catholicism is presented as an integral part of the speaker's identity and the comfort of religion is like the comfort of family: 'candles soothed the bedside' in 'Mid-Term Break' and the rosary is part of the daily routine in 'The Other Side'. Elements of Catholicism also provide a vocabulary for exploring other experiences, often of a more sexual nature. For example, the healing of the rift in 'Summer Home' is effected by means of 'a May altar of sorts', the speaker cries out 'Anoint the wound' and, as she bends in the shower, 'water lives down the tilting stoups of [her] breasts' (a stoup is a basin for holy water). The skunk, which comes to represent the sexually desirable wife, has a tail like a chasuble (the priest's outer vestment). There even could be something innocently erotic about the relationship between the young speaker and his mother in 'Clearances' during their '*Sons and Lovers* phase' when they were 'Elbow to elbow' and 'glad to be kneeling next/ To each other up there near the front/ Of the packed church'.

Other poems present Catholicism unfavourably. 'Limbo' raises the question of severe interpretations of scripture, in which the unbaptised child is condemned to a temporary hell. 'Sweeney in Connacht' shows the outcast treated unfairly by a mean-spirited cleric who refuses refuge or sustenance. As Sweeney responds, harsh stresses fall on 'bell-man' and 'monk' so that they sound like curses, and the mad king has to question him directly to make him see things from a perspective other than his own. By the time we reach the pilgrimage of 'Station Island', paradoxically, belief in Catholicism seems to have faded. The speaker goes through some of the rites in a dilatory fashion and several of the characters either cast doubt on the faith or the poet seems to be satirising it through them. The first character is the 'Sabbath-breaker', Simon Sweeney, who exclaims 'Stay clear of all processions!' and the second is Carlton who uses the term 'holy Jesus Christ' as a way to swear rather than a subject of adoration. The priest who appears in Section IV seems like an anachronism and is perhaps presented as someone whose life has been wasted for the pride of others. He doesn't seem to have fitted in: either in the missions, where the locals still follow their more primitive religions, or at home, where he is a 'holy mascot', and spends his time 'Drinking tea and praising home-made bread'.

In *The Haw Lantern*, there seems to be a wider loss of faith. While 'The Spoonbait' presents the full ridiculousness of religious indoctrination in a comical fashion, 'The Mud Vision' suggests that with the loss of religion comes a vacuum that modern life fails to fill. 'From the Republic of Conscience' perhaps draws on the Republic of Ireland where the politicians, through their lack of conscience have failed in their duty to those whose trust they abuse and whose taxes they spend.

The poet's methods

Target your thinking

- Consider the different methods that Heaney uses in *New Selected Poems*: which are the most important in each poem. How are they used to shape meaning and to create effects? (**AO2**)
- As you consider methods and meaning, note uses of literary terms; how can you use literary terminology to help you to articulate your responses with more precision and concision? (**AO1**)
- How might your understanding of poetic methods help you to make connections with your comparative set text (if relevant to your exam board)? (**AO4**)
- In what ways can different close readings lead to alternative interpretations? (**AO5**)

Variety

While some readers might think of the early rural work, or the later bog poetry as being quintessential Heaney, the truth is that his poetry is incredibly versatile. Within *New Selected Poems* there is a diverse range of forms as well as techniques. There are prose poems and dramatic poems, elegies, dramatic monologues, allegories, translations, satires and sonnets. Above all, there are lyric poems, that is, those that express the thoughts and feelings of a single speaker in a subjective manner, meditating and reflecting on events and sometimes coming to conclusions or expanding to broader concerns.

Taking it further ▶

Make a list of all the poems that are sonnets, then comment closely on the different ways in which Heaney uses that form.

TASK

Take the following subgenres of lyric as headings: elegy, dramatic monologue, love lyric and sonnet. Place poems from *New Selected Poems* in the appropriate categories. How does thinking about each poem in the context of its subgenre contribute to your response?

CRITICAL VIEW

Helen Vendler opposes critics who quarrel with Heaney's poems, saying: 'To read lyric poems as if they were expository essays is a fundamental philosophical mistake' (Vendler 2000, p.9). In your own words, explain what she means; give examples from specific poems that might be interpreted politically as you do so.

Contexts

Target your thinking

- How does contextual material help you to deepen your understanding of the poems? (**AO1**)
- In what ways can you apply contextual readings or critical approaches to the poems? (**AO3**)
- How does contextual understanding help you to make connections? (**AO4**)
- In what ways might your understanding of contexts lead you to consider alternative interpretations? (**AO5**)

Biographical context

Seamus Heaney was born in 1939, the eldest of nine children. He grew up on his father's farm in County Derry, Northern Ireland. The landscape of his boyhood influences many of his poems. The influence of his family can be felt too. His relationship with his quiet father is foregrounded poems such as 'Follower' and 'The Stone Verdict' and his more forthcoming mother is memorialised in 'Clearances'. His Aunt Mary, who lived with the Heaneys, was like a second mother and her loving presence is commemorated in 'Mossbawn: Two Poems in Dedication'.

An outstanding student, Heaney learnt Latin in primary school and won a scholarship to board at St Columb's College in the city of Derry. Later, he got a first in English at Queen's University, Belfast. His journey from the farm to the lecture theatre can be seen in poems from 'Digging' to 'Alphabets'. Soon after graduating, while working as a teacher, Heaney began writing poetry and met other young poets, including Derek Mahon and Michael Longley, at a poetry workshop that became known as the Group. Chaired by Philip Hobsbaum, an academic at Queen's, these meetings were said to engender rivalry, companionship and, ultimately, some wonderful poetry. (For more about the Group, see Literary contexts, p.86.)

Heaney's first collection, *Death of a Naturalist* appeared in 1966. Not long after it had been accepted by Faber & Faber, Heaney married Marie Devlin. His experiences of marriage – its joys and its frustrations – are drawn on in many of his poems: from 'Wedding Day' to 'A Dream of Jealousy' and from 'The Skunk' to 'The Underground'

Heaney lectured at Queen's University while continuing to write and, in 1969, published *Door into the Dark*. This was also the year in which the conflict known as the Troubles began to flare. The tension between the poetic responsibility to

▲ Seamus Heaney

address the concerns of his society and the need to avoid being inflammatory or propagandist runs through Heaney's work. In 1972 he published *Wintering Out* in which political tensions are reflected with varying degrees of directness. The collection includes his first poems to use preserved Iron Age bodies to explore violence in Northern Ireland.

In the same year, to dedicate himself more fully to writing, Heaney resigned his lectureship and relocated to an isolated cottage in County Wicklow. In 1973, he visited Copenhagen and met P.V. Glob, the author of *The Bog People*, and his next collection, *North* (1975), confronted aspects of the violence in Northern Ireland in imaginative and provocative ways, including making extensive metaphorical use of bog bodies. It remains his most controversial collection. In 1976, Heaney moved to Dublin, where he began work as a lecturer in English in Carysfort College of Education. This offered security to his family and the post also enabled him to take up a term as visiting professor at the University of California. The duties were relatively light and, he said, allowed him to live in the country in his mind.

Field Work (1979) reflects some of the artistic liberation afforded by the Wicklow years and includes elegies for people known to him who died as a consequence of the Troubles. In 1981 Heaney became a director of Field Day, a group of artists and writers whose aim was to introduce what they termed 'a fifth province'. It would be in addition to the four physical provinces of Ireland and be a province of the mind – a place where the 'colonial crisis' in Northern Ireland could be explored. He also took up a teaching post at Harvard University, which only required him to teach poetry workshops in the spring term and left him free to write for the rest of the year.

When Heaney was included in *The Penguin Book of Contemporary British Poetry* (1983) he responded with a satirical verse epistle, 'An Open Letter', rejecting the term 'British'. *Sweeney Astray*, a book of dramatic monologues translated from Irish, in the persona of a mad king who was transformed into a bird, appeared in 1983. The medieval Irish king reappeared in 'Sweeney Redivivus', the final sequence of Heaney's next collection, *Station Island* (1984). These take more liberties with the source material and make more overt use of autobiography. The collection marks another stage in the poet's artistic development as it engages with elements of his past, interrogates the idea of the poet's responsibilities head on and makes greater use of drama and direct speech.

Heaney's mother died in 1984 and his father in 1986. Such losses are felt in *The Haw Lantern* (1987), along with loss in a wider sense, such as loss of faith in religion and politics. The collection contains parable poems and satires, and the work, while often about Ireland, has a broader and more international reach. His next collection, *Seeing Things* (1991), also seems less rooted and more concerned with the spiritual. It appealed to a wide audience. The lyrical beauty and ethical depth of his work were recognised in 1995 when he won the highest honour in world literature, the Nobel Prize.

Heaney continued to garner a great many prizes, including becoming Professor of Poetry at Oxford (1999) and winning the Whitbread Book of the Year Award for his

Literary contexts

The Group

This was the name given to a poetry workshop that Heaney attended after graduating.

Other young poets who attended included Derek Mahon and Michael Longley, and the Group was chaired by Philip Hobsbaum, a poet and a lecturer at Queen's. The products of these workshops were said to be rivalry, companionship and, ultimately, some wonderful poetry. Heaney later implied that some of his work engendered jealousy among the group.

Language

Heaney's work is preoccupied with language. For example, 'Afterwards' evokes his learning of English, Irish and Greek. His early writing is sometimes compared to that of Patrick Kavanagh. Heaney wrote about Kavanagh's poetry in his essay 'A Placeless Heaven', which explains the importance of a writer having a sense of place and knowing where he comes from: to truly know the parish is to know the world. Heaney's feeling for the Irish language is also evident in poems such as 'Stations of the West' and in his extensive use of the Sweeney poems. Yet English writing is also a prized part of his heritage. For example, his love of Anglo-Saxon poetry is well documented, and his affinity with the Romantics, especially Wordsworth and Keats, comes through in some of his early poems.

In his later work, Heaney was influenced by Eastern European writers such as Czeslaw Milosz, some of whose poems use parables as a way to avoid censorship. In addition, Heaney's love of the Classics is an important context. From *Field Work* onwards, many of his poems depend on the reader recognising – or being willing to research – references to Greek mythology.

The poet as critic

As well as being a pre-eminent poet, Heaney is a thoughtful and insightful critic. His analysis of English-speaking poets such as Kavanagh, Auden and Plath, as well as Eastern European poets such as Osip Mandelstam can be read in *Preoccupations*, *The Government of the Tongue* and *Finders Keepers*, his book of selected prose which won the Truman Capote Award in 2003. It is worth paying attention to what he admires in other writers and considering the extent to which his own poetry shares those features. Heaney's critical stance is largely that of a New Critic combined with Historicism. He has said that he regards critical theory (deriving from thinkers such as Jacques Derrida) as being detrimental to literature and scholarship. That said, it is interesting to consider the ways in which some of his writing reflects aspects of postmodernism, for example, poems like 'The Mud Vision' which is an interesting mix of narrative, allusions and references to high and low culture.

Taking it further ▶

Heaney's contemporaries and the poets preceding his generation might also be seen as influences on his work. You might like to research Robert Lowell and Ted Hughes and consider the extent to which knowing about such influences casts light on your reading of *New Selected Poems*. O'Driscoll's book of interviews, *Stepping Stones*, is a good starting point. It also gives interesting details about the influence of Eastern European writers on Heaney.

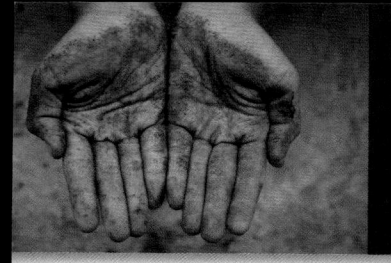

Working with the text

Assessment Objectives and skills

> **AO1** Articulate informed, personal and creative responses to literary texts, using associated concepts and terminology, and coherent, accurate written expression.

To do well with AO1 you need to write fluently, structuring your essay carefully, guiding your reader clearly through your line of argument and using the sophisticated vocabulary, including critical terminology, which is appropriate to an A-level essay. You will need to use frequent embedded quotations to show detailed knowledge and demonstrate familiarity with the whole text. Your aim is to produce a well-written academic essay employing appropriate discourse markers to create the sense of a shaped argument. It should use sophisticated terminology at times while remaining clear and cohesive.

> **AO2** Analyse ways in which meanings are shaped in literary texts.

Strong students do not work only on a lexical level, but write well on the generic and structural elements of the poems in *New Selected Poems*, so it is useful to start by analysing those larger elements of narrative organisation before considering the poets' use of language. If 'form is meaning', what are the implications of this for each poem? Then again, to discuss language in detail you will need to quote from poems, analyse what you quote and use it to illuminate your argument. Since you will at times need to make points about generic and organisational features of the text much too long to quote in full, being able to reference closely and effectively is just as important as mastering the art of the embedded quotation. Practise writing in analytical sentences, comprising a brief quotation or close reference, a definition or description of the feature you intend to analyse, an explanation of how this feature has been used and an evaluation of its effects.

> **AO3** Demonstrate understanding of the significance and influence of the contexts in which literary texts are written and received.

To access AO3 you need to think about how contexts of production, reception, literature, culture, biography, geography, society, history, genre and intertextuality can affect texts. Place each poem at the heart of a web of contextual factors which you feel have had the most impact upon it; examiners want to see a sense of contextual alertness woven seamlessly into the fabric of your essay rather than a clumsy bolted-on website rehash or some recycled history notes. Show you understand that literary works contain encoded representations of the cultural, moral, religious, racial and political values of the society from which they emerged, and that over time attitudes and ideas change until the views they reflect are no longer widely shared.

> **AO4** Explore connections across literary texts.

If your examination requires you to compare and contrast one or more other texts with *New Selected Poems* you must try to find specific points of comparison, rather than merely generalising. You will find it easier to make connections between texts (of any kind) if you balance them as you write; remember also that connections are not only about finding similarities – differences are just as interesting. Above all, consider how the comparison illuminates each text; some connections will be thematic, others generic or stylistic.

> **AO5** Explore literary texts informed by different interpretations.

For this AO, you should refer to the opinions of critics and remain alert to aspects of the poems which are open to interpretation. Your job is to measure your own interpretation of the text against those of other readers. Try to convey an awareness of multiple readings as well as an understanding that (as Barthes suggested) a text's meaning is dependent as much upon what you bring to it as what the poet left there. Using modal verb phrases such as 'may be seen as', 'might be interpreted as' or 'could be represented as' shows you know that different readers interpret texts in different ways at different times. The key word here is plurality; there is no single meaning or one right answer. Relish getting your teeth into the views of published critics to push forward your own argument, but always keep in mind that meanings in poems are shifting and unstable as opposed to fixed and permanent.

Summary

Overall, the hallmarks of a successful A-level essay that hits all five AOs include:

- a clear introduction that orientates the reader and outlines your main argument
- a coherent and conceptualised argument that relates to the question title
- confident movement around the text rather than a relentless chronological trawl through it
- apt and effective quotations or references adapted to make sense within the context of your own sentence
- a range of effective points about Heaney's methods

- a strong and personally engaged awareness of how a text can be interpreted by different readers and audiences in different ways at different times
- a sense that you are prepared to take on a good range of critical and theoretical perspectives
- a conclusion that effectively summarises and consolidates your response and relates it back to your essay title.

Top quotations

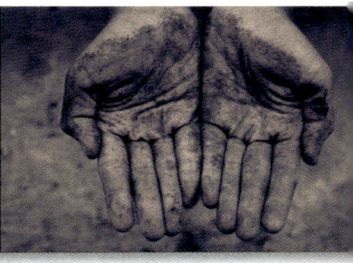

Before studying this section, you should identify your own 'top quotations'. Choose those that are rich in poetic methods and give you plenty of scope for further comment, and/or that seem to capture a key theme or aspect of the poem or collection aptly and memorably. Identify clearly what it is about your choices that makes each one so significant. No two people studying Seamus Heaney's *New Selected Poems 1966–1987* will select exactly the same set, and it will be well worth comparing and defending your choices with the other students in your class. In addition, because there are so many poems to choose from, with such rich and varied styles and subjects, you might want to expand the task and select a top fifteen or a top twenty. For that reason, this guide lists a baker's dozen of 13 quotations rather than the usual ten.

When you have done this, look carefully at the following list of quotations and consider each one's possible significance within the poem and/or the collection from which it comes. Discuss the ways in which each might be used in an essay to support your exploration of various elements of *New Selected Poems 1966–1987*. Consider what each quotation tells us about Seamus Heaney's ideas, themes and methods, as well as how far it may contribute to various potential ways of interpreting the text.

1

Between my finger and my thumb
The squat pen rests.
I'll dig with it.

From 'Digging' in *Death of Naturalist*

- This quotation from what Heaney regards as his first real poem offers an interesting introduction to some of the issues that preoccupy his work in general. Writing, tradition and breaking with tradition are all suggested by the spade/pen image as are ideas around violence. The pen was 'snug as a gun' in the second line of the first stanza, and by this conclusion we might say that the speaker has vowed to take up the pen rather than the gun. Indeed, Heaney might be suggesting that he is refusing to use his pen for overt political comment or to support a political cause. The quotation returns to almost the same two lines with which the poem began. But instead of giving readers the half-rhyme of 'thumb' and 'gun' that they might have expected, the poem's penultimate line breaks the couplet by stopping the second line halfway through. Heaney leaves a half line ending in 'rests' and places the last part of the line (two iambic feet) on the final line. This places more emphasis on 'rests', which is now end-stopped and the last word of the line. As well as meaning positioned or sitting, 'rests' might also suggest a break after a period of activity. Perhaps this implies that the poet is going to be a ruminative writer who allows himself thinking time as he composes, rather than one who will write to order or in the heat of the moment.

The quotation has the descriptive power and some of the sensuousness associated with early Heaney. The close up description of the pen's position and its 'squat' shape brings the feeling of holding it alive and the conclusion of the poem surprises the reader with its abrupt flight from the naturalistic to the metaphorical as the speaker make a simple four word, monosyllabic vow: 'I'll dig with it'. This metaphorical digging is not just an alternative to real digging (with a spade such as his father and grandfather did) but digging in the sense of excavation: into such areas as history, culture and language. It is also a vow to question, seek and explore. The poetry that follows is not going to be work of someone with fixed ideas, but one who, with his pen, will enquire, consider and investigate. He will ask plenty of questions – of himself and the reader – but may not provide easy answers.

2

Until, on Vinegar Hill, the fatal conclave.
Terraced thousands died, shaking scythes at cannon.
The hillside blushed, soaked in our broken wave.
They buried us without shroud or coffin
And in August the barley grew up out of the grave.

From 'Requiem for the Croppies' in *Door into the Dark*

- The conclusion of this sonnet makes an abject defeat sound like a moment of defiance and triumph. In the final line, time shifts: the barley that the rebels of 1798 carried in their pockets as they went into battle has taken root and grown in the soil where they were buried. Note the poetic effects that make their actions and living legacy seem attractive. The point of view – the first person plural – encourages us to identify with the rebels as we hear their story directly from the mouth of an unnamed rebel who speaks for them all. There is a pleasing cyclical effect as the barley that was a simple and portable meal in line one returns in the final line, perhaps as a fitting natural monument to the rebels as well as to suggest the flourishing of their ideals. Three full rhymes draw attention to this shift in how the rebels are presented: from the 'fatal conclave' (in the two lines above the quotation) – to the 'broken wave' to, lastly, the 'barley that grew up out of the grave'. As well as a meeting (in this case of armies), the word 'conclave' can mean a meeting of cardinals in the Catholic Church, so there is perhaps a sense of holiness and righteousness about the rebels' cause. The 'broken wave' could refer to the advance of the rebels that the British crushed, but it might also suggest the volume of bloodshed involved – the hillside that is personified as having 'blushed' has been soaked in a wave of rebel blood. As well as turning red with the amount of rebel blood that 'soaked' into it, the blush might be read as the embarrassment of nature at the waste caused by this terrible defeat and the unfair and inhumane ways in which it was meted out to the rebels, who faced cannon with farm tools and were buried without funeral rites. Yet with the organic imagery of growth in the final lines, the mood has shifted to admiration and joy at the memories of the rebels and their ideals living on. The sonnet itself – which might also be considered as an elegy – is perhaps compensating for the lack of ceremony surrounding the deaths of the rebels at the time by providing, as its title indicates, a requiem for the croppies. The sense of fitting commemoration is strong politically, particularly when we remember that the poem was written on the fiftieth anniversary of the 1916 Easter Rising. It is easy to argue that the sonnet suggests that the seeds of 1916 were planted in 1798. An oppositional reading of the poem is to suggest that it glorifies blood sacrifice. While this may not have been the poet's intention, it could be argued that its sense of glorifying dying for the cause of a united Ireland free from British intervention, plays into the hands of Republicans. Here, the context of reception is important and we might remember that an illegal recording of the poem was used on a compilation of rebel songs and that Heaney, not wishing to be associated with any overt political cause, stopped performing the poem at public readings.

3

Anahorish, soft gradient
of consonant, vowel-meadow,

From 'Anahorish' in *Wintering Out*

- These lines are the poetic saying aloud of a place-name; in this case, the village where Heaney went to primary school. The italicised word is pronounced aloud and the speaker luxuriates in the sound of the name as well as the actual place. There is also a sense that the place-name is not arbitrary, but that it embodies something of the place itself. Thus the poem might be read in the context of the Irish *dinnseanchas* tradition in which the name of the place encapsulates the character of the place. Note also how the poet's literary and rural sensibilities are united in the poem. The place is celebrated, but through grammatical terms. The slope of the land is like the two initial consonant sounds – the 'n' and the 'h' – yet these consonants are not harsh, but gentle. The 'o' in the middle of the word is like the expanse of meadow (a piece of grassland, typically used for making hay) in Anahorish. It produces a long soft sound as the place-name is said, and the final sounds are also soft and open, with even the consonant 'r' being soft and vowel-like and the final 'sh' sound providing the place-name with a pleasing sibilant finish.

The poetic saying aloud expresses the speaker's identification with – even sense of ownership of – the place. We remember that he said it was 'my place' in the first line as he translated the place-name as 'place of clear water'. There is also an innocence to the poem, which has a prelapsarian feel. It is untroubled by any elements of threat or invasion and is useful to contrast with 'Broagh' and other poems in which the Irish landscape is contested.

But now I stand behind him
in the dark yard, in the moan of prayers.
He puts a hand in a pocket

or taps a little tune with the blackthorn
shyly, as if he were party to
lovemaking or a stranger's weeping.

Should I slip away, I wonder,
or go up and touch his shoulder
and talk about the weather

or the price of grass-seed?

From 'The Other Side' in *Wintering Out*

> ▼ The title of this poem is a way of referring to Protestants by Catholics and vice versa, but while it might suggest sensitivity in not naming them by their religion, it could also suggest ignorance in that it treats all of those from one religion as a single group, suggesting that they are all the same. In addition, it casts the other religion as the 'other': that which is different from, distinct from or opposite to, and which carries a sense of strangeness.
>
> The quotation is the conclusion to the third and final section of the poem. It has followed a short second section in which the speaker reported his household making fun of their Protestant neighbour. In this final section, a more nuanced and thoughtful version of the Protestant neighbour is presented. The speaker is in the yard behind him while he waits respectfully for the Catholic prayers (being said by the rest of the family) to be concluded before he knocks. Note how the tense has changed. From the habitual mood of 'would' – the Protestant neighbour would do this and that – which lumps his behaviours and the Catholic family's mocking of them together as being typical and places both in the past, the narrative shifts to the present tense and to a greater degree of detail and specificity.

The speaker notices the Protestant neighbour's actions and perhaps sees him less as 'other' and begins to appreciate things from his perspective. With 'the moan of prayers' it is the behaviour of the family inside that perhaps seems strange rather than Protestant's actions. The speaker picks up on his gestures: the 'hand in a pocket', the way he 'taps a little tune' with his stick and finds equivalent experiences that would produce similar embarrassment, such as intruding on a stranger weeping. The tone has become serious and, in the final four lines, embarrassment and indecision are experienced by the speaker. They contain three potential actions expressed as a question: should he 'slip away', talk about the weather or 'the price of grass seed'? Note how uncertainty is emphasised through rhyme. The penultimate stanza is a triplet – 'wonder', 'shoulder' and 'weather' are all half-rhymes – and this is prominent in an otherwise unrhymed poem, drawing attention to this climax of embarrassment and indecision. The final line breaks the poem's pattern of three-line stanzas and concludes it with a single-line stanza that completes the questions started in the penultimate stanza. Perhaps it communicates a sense of the speaker wanting to find an easy way to talk to his Protestant neighbour, or just his desperate desire to find a way out of this embarrassing situation.

5

here is a space
again, the scone rising
to the tick of two clocks.

And here is love
like a tinsmith's scoop
sunk past its gleam
in the meal-bin.

From 'Mossbawn: Two Poems in Dedication *For Mary Heaney*:
I *Sunlight*' in *North*

> The quotation is the final part of the first poem in *North*, 'Sunlight'. It conveys the atmosphere of calm in the kitchen after the homely activity of baking when there is space to wait for the scones to rise. While the poem is dedicated to Heaney's aunt, Mary, who lived with the family and whom we imagine as the subject who bakes in the poem, the 'tick of two clocks' might be read symbolically to mean both sources of order and care in the family home: Heaney's mother and his aunt. On one level, this is a homely image of an excess of love and care, with the two clocks, like the two women they symbolise in harmony. On another, some readers might wonder if, in the subtext, there is a hint of tension, or potential tension, between the two women of the household. It is, after all, unnecessary and possibly confusing, to time the baking of scones with two clocks.

Top quotations

The final quatrain extrapolates from the details of baking to explore the importance of what has been described. The descriptions, for the speaker, evoke love. Note the prominence of the word love at the end of the first line of the last stanza. It is a word that Heaney seldom uses and is careful about using, and thus its rarity lends it increased power. The simile that follows is a traditional and homely one. Love is like 'a tinsmith's scoop' sunk in a meal-bin. Perhaps the scoop being 'sunk past its gleam' suggests that it is buried deeply in the grain and only part of it can be seen. This might suggest that the love is so deep it can't be seen completely: much of it is below the surface. It is also something that extends beyond the shiny 'gleam' of newness, but is solid, ongoing and sustaining.

6

I who have stood dumb
when your betraying sisters,
cauled in tar,
wept by the railings,

who would connive
in civilised outrage
yet understand the exact
and tribal, intimate revenge.

From 'Punishment' in *North*

- The quotation comes from the end of one of Heaney's most controversial poems. The speaker has admitted that he is an 'artful voyeur' and he is examining the complexities of his feelings, both towards the victims and the perpetrators of the punishment. (In the first part of the poem the punishment appeared to be the ritual death given to an Iron Age woman for adultery, but in the final part, the imagery of the Iron Age blends into that of 1970s Northern Ireland. In this context, the punishment is given to a Catholic woman being tarred and feathered as a public humiliation for going out with a British soldier.) Once again, Heaney's speaker is able to explore complexities, but seems unwilling or unable to take a firm viewpoint or to act: he simply 'stood dumb'.

  The final stanza explores the complexities of his conflicting thoughts and feelings overtly. He would be both outraged at the violence and understand the feelings of those who are responsible for it. On one level, this might be seen as the speaker, or even the poet, trying to have it both ways and avoid taking sides, which some critics, such as Edna Longley, have found distasteful. On another, it might be said that he is revealing honest, if troubling, feelings. What he does not want to do is to simply 'connive/ in civilised outrage'. Civilised outrage might seem a reasonable response, but to 'connive' is to secretly allow something harmful, immoral or illegal to happen. Simply to show outrage might be to mouth platitudes similar those such as 'Oh, it's disgraceful, surely, I agree' from 'Whatever You Say Say Nothing'. Instead, what the speaker does is expose himself by risking the sharing of real feelings that a Catholic might have in response to such a situation in the heat of the worst times of the Troubles rather than self-censor and write what might seem palatable. This might be linked to Heaney's nuanced explorations of responses to the IRA in 'Badgers', for example, when he hears 'intimations whispered/ about being vaguely honoured'. The final lines of 'Punishment' perhaps seem the most heartfelt and brutally honest of the poem and they have the artistic merit of bringing the poem to a powerful climax and merging both of its narratives – from the Iron Age and the Northern Ireland Conflict. The speaker doesn't say he approves of the violent punishment, but he does admit that he understands it: 'the exact/ and tribal, intimate revenge'.

7
I dab you clean with moss
Fine as the drizzle out of a low cloud.
I lift you under the arms and lay you flat.
With rushes that shoot green again, I plait
Green scapulars to wear over your shroud.

From 'The Strand at Lough Beg' in *Field Work*

The poem is an elegy for Column McCartney, a second cousin of Heaney who wasn't known to him personally. McCartney was shot dead by Loyalist terrorists in a random attack. The elegy is a public poem that is expressed in formal, elevated language and at the close it offers consolation by alluding to a moment in Dante's *The Divine Comedy*, when Virgil washes the poet Dante, cleaning his face with the dews of Purgatory and cleansing it free from the dirt of Hell. Thus Heaney offers a sense of the sacred and ritual to the man whose life was taken in such an unholy way. Note the solemn, mournful and respectful tone as the speaker addresses the dead man directly and the abundance of consoling natural imagery as he describes his actions – he lifts his dead cousin up, lays him out respectfully, then plaits bulrushes around him which form scapulars over his shroud. Since a scapular is both a type of bandage passed over and around the shoulders and a type of monk's cloak, there is a sense of both healing and holiness in the speaker's actions.

Consider the formal aspects of the elegy. It is written in regular lines of iambic pentameter and uses an intricate rhyme scheme. In this final sequence of the speaker washing the dead man with dew and wrapping his body with bulrushes, note the use of envelope rhyme. The line that ends with 'the drizzle out of a low cloud' rhymes with the line that ends with 'scapulars to wear over your shroud'. In the middle of this enveloping rhyme is a couplet whose lines end with 'lay you flat' and 'again, I plait'. Perhaps this technique helps the actions of the central couplet to stay in the reader's mind longer, or perhaps it simply adds further adornment to the poem, helping to add to the artistic beauty of the elegy that is offered as a tribute to the dead man. Before considering the ways in which the ideas of this poem are repudiated in 'Station Island', it is worth remembering that many readers find it, and these lines in particular, among the most beautiful and moving in Heaney's work.

8

Up, black, striped and damasked like the chasuble
At a funeral mass, the skunk's tail
Paraded the skunk.

From 'The Skunk' in *Field Work*

- This masterful description is from the opening of 'The Skunk' – a poem that performs the unlikely feat of taking a small animal known primarily for its offensive smell and turning it into an emblem of love. Note the pace of the first line, with the caesurae and plosive consonants ('u**p**, **b**lack, stri**p**ed') mimicking the quick, jerky movements of the skunk. Consider also how the tail is described first. This is apt as the tail is prominent, bushy and the most obvious thing about the creature; you are likely to notice its tail before its body. The tail seems almost alive – it 'paraded' the skunk – and this is apt in a poem that explores sexual desire and sexual display. It also prepares us for the poem's final image that makes the skunk/woman analogy overt as the poet savours the image of his wife:
Your head-down, tail-up hunt in a bottom drawer
For the black plunge-line nightdress.

9

The end of art is peace
Could be the motto of this frail device
That I have pinned up on our deal dresser –
Like a drawn snare
Slipped lately by the spirit of the corn
Yet burnished by its passage, and still warm.

From 'The Harvest Bow' in *Field Work*

- The poem is notable for its use of multivalent symbolism. The harvest bow might symbolise several things such as love, the relationship between father and son or respect for the spirit of the harvest. Yet towards the end of the poem, the speaker is explicit and suggests that the saying that it expresses might be '*the end of art is peace*'. At first this seems quite a high-minded maxim for a simple bow fashioned from left over harvest straw to express. But perhaps the peace meant is more localised. Rather than peace in a country that has been at war, might the peace in question be that which comes from making peace with the past, or achieving peace of mind, or even the peace felt in the countryside? Note how the idealism of the bow's motto is diluted in the second line of the stanza: it only 'could' be the bow's motto; and the bow itself is only a 'frail device'. The speaker cares enough about the harvest bow to use it as an ornament, pinned 'on our deal dresser', but undermines this thought with the simile that follows. The harvest bow is 'Like a drawn snare' (an open trap) – which is a thought amplified by its prominent position as a single line, the shortest of the poem, comprised of only four monosyllables. The poem concludes with a strong sense of the harvest bow's power, connecting it to ancient customs and superstitions. It has escaped from 'the spirit of the corn' and is both 'burnished' and 'still warm'. The verb 'burnished' is means brightened, or perfected. Not often used today, the word usually applies to metals that are shined by means of rubbing; it carries connotations of gleaming weapons, thus lending the bow powerful, impressive and beautiful qualities beyond those which we might associate with such a light and flimsy substance as straw. This is added to by the thermal image of it being 'warm', with the glow of its warmth perhaps being suggested in the masculine rhyme with corn from the previous line. Thus, the poem ends with a strong sense of the harvest bow's traditional and mysterious power.

You might like to consider the poem as a development from early father and son poems such as 'Digging'. Unlike such poems from *Death of a Naturalist*, the nature of the relationships and the feelings are not spelled out in 'The Harvest Bow'. The sense of the continuity of rural traditions and of the son's distance from them are presented more subtly, through subtext and implication rather than overtly. Similarly, there is a strong sense of love between father and son in the poem, and even though this is unstated, it is no less palpable.

10

'You saw that, and you wrote that – not the fact.
You confused evasion and artistic tact.
The Protestant who shot me through the head
I accuse directly, but indirectly, you
who now atone perhaps upon this bed
for the way you whitewashed ugliness and drew
the lovely blinds of the *Purgatorio*
and saccharined my death with morning dew.'

From Section VIII of 'Station Island' in *Station Island*

- Heaney makes use of dialogue and dramatic conflict in this section from 'Station Island'. Stylistically it is the antithesis of 'The Strand at Lough Beg' and it offers a completely different slant on the death of Colum McCartney and how it should be remembered. The speaker here is McCartney himself and he argues vigorously and angrily with a version of Heaney. Note the way in which he jabs at him directly with the second person pronoun 'you'. There is no room for evasion or excuses; the second cousin is very clear about what Heaney did and the error of his actions. He sees the Heaney figure's pilgrimage to Lough Derg as a selfish attempt to be redeemed for his artistic misrepresentation. McCartney's words are forthright. He treats the elegiac features of Heaney's former writing with contempt, seeing them as dishonest and distorting: 'You whitewashed ugliness' – that is, made it seem pretty and covered it up dishonestly. Sarcasm is added as describes the 'lovely blinds of the *Purgatorio*'. The blinds are on one level coming down in respect for the dead, but on another might be seen as concealing or masking. The idea of the death being 'saccharined' presumably refers to Heaney making it sweet and palatable for his readers, possibly even playing to his educated audience, making literary capital out of the death and writing in a manner that would not be appreciated by the supposed primary audience – the dead man himself.

  While it is possible to read the poem from a purely autobiographical angle, it is also interesting to read it in the light of contemporary events in Northern Ireland. It was being written during the time of the hunger strikes, a period of the Troubles that saw an increasing polarisation of Catholics and Protestants as well as a rise in support for the IRA. Notice how the voice of McCartney doesn't distinguish type of person who murdered him: he is not considered as a Loyalist, or a terrorist; he is referred to simply as a Protestant.

11

In the margin of texts of praise
they scratched and clawed.
They snarled if the day was dark
or too much chalk had made the vellum bland
or too little left it oily.

From 'The Scribes' in 'Sweeney Redivivus' in *Station Island*

- It is worth remembering that the poem is actually in the persona of the mad Irish poet, Sweeney, rather than in the voice of Heaney. It is commensurate with what we know of Sweeney's character in the other poems in that he voices complaints. That said, this poem is also a looser use of the original Irish material than Heaney's earlier Sweeney collection *Sweeney Astray*, so as well as referring to Sweeney's mistreatment at the hands of other monks who also work with chalk and vellum, it engages with Heaney's own critics and rivals. There is also something comical about the way these monkish figures praise, yet cannot help allowing their jealousy to bubble up in the form of virulent criticism. Note the use of animal verbs as they 'scratched and clawed' and 'snarled'. Their criticisms are presented as being mean-spirited and petty, and rather than voice them openly, they are aired in 'the margins'.

This poem also marks Heaney's renewed self-confidence in his work. After the cathartic journey of 'Station Island', he seems to have grown more relaxed and at ease with himself. Rather than absorb criticism, here he hits back satirically.

12

so you end up scrutinized from behind the haw
he holds up at eye-level on its twig,
and you flinch before its bonded pith and stone,
its blood-prick that you wish would test and clear you,
its pecked-at ripeness that scans you, then moves on.

From 'The Haw Lantern' in *The Haw Lantern*

'The Haw Lantern' is a parable-like poem that is remarkable for its transforming imagery and its simple, arresting power. The figure in the poem is not from contemporary Ireland, but ancient Greece. Diogenes is the philosopher who has rejected society and devoted himself to a search for truth. The poem places the reader in the perspective of one being scrutinised by him as he holds up his lantern in the light of day, searching for a just man in the marketplace. Diogenes' lantern is the red fruit of the hawthorn tree, which is described in detail in the quotation. It has transformed from the 'small light for small people' that it was in the first stanza to something powerful and unusual: it makes 'you flinch' as its brightness moves close. Heaney uses the metaphor of the thumb prick blood test to suggest the severity and thoroughness of being scrutinised by Diogenes and his lantern. The verb 'scans' continues the medical/scientific sense of the test as well as its seriousness, before the surprising implication that the test is failed and that the reader, like most people, suffers from the disease of dishonesty or unjustness. Note how the disappointment of the conclusion is gently underscored by sound and rhythm. The feminine ending of the last line (it ends on an unstressed syllable) has a falling quality and sounds a mournful note. This is reinforced by half-rhyme (between 'and stone' and 'moves on') – which stands out as the only use of rhyme in the poem. It is also interesting structurally. Heaney does not move from the particular to the general, or from a specific experience to drawing wider conclusions as he does elsewhere. For example, in 'Digging' the speaker observes his father digging, explores memories and develops thoughts and feelings before concluding that he will dig with his pen. In 'The Haw Lantern' Heaney begins with general details and ends with a specific experience without spelling out conclusions overtly. Heaney's use of the third and second person has written the speaker/poet figure out of the poem, forcing the reader to draw his or her own conclusions and to scrutinise their own morality.

13

I remembered her head bent towards my head,
Her breath in mine, our fluent dipping knives –
Never closer the whole rest of our lives.

From 'Clearances 3' in *The Haw Lantern*

> Straight away, you can feel the differences in terms of sound and sense between this quotation and the previous one (from 'The Haw Lantern'). It is from an autobiographical sonnet in 'Clearances' – an elegy in the form of a sonnet sequence that celebrates and commemorates the life of Heaney's mother. The rhythm is regular iambic pentameter (if we read 'towards' as monosyllabic – 't'wards' – as it is often pronounced in Ulster) and the couplet forms a satisfying full rhyme. This pleasing sound is reinforced and seems uplifting (rather than downcast, as the rhyme was at the end of 'The Haw Lantern') since the couplet has a masculine rhyme (the rhyme is between two stressed syllables) that sounds a conclusive note. The experience is clear, direct and homely: the speaker and his mother peel potatoes together in contented silence, while the rest of the family has gone to Mass. Consider also the use of perspective. The quotation begins with the first person reminiscence, but, in the couplet, the memory is not so much the speaker's memory of his mother, but his memory of them being together. There is a deep sense of togetherness too in Heaney's language. Their work has symmetry and harmony: their heads are bent together, their knives work together and they breathe together. 'Her breath in mine' suggests an intimacy and closeness that is usually reserved for lovers, and the poem concludes by underlining the significance of this experience as being the time when mother and son were most close. In addition, the gentle power of this remembered communion between mother and son contrasts sharply with the official rites of the Catholic church, when the impersonal-sounding 'parish priest' went 'hammer and tongs at the prayers for the dying'. The speaker's memory seems to remove him from that experience and the grief of recent bereavement, by transporting him to a place of contentment.

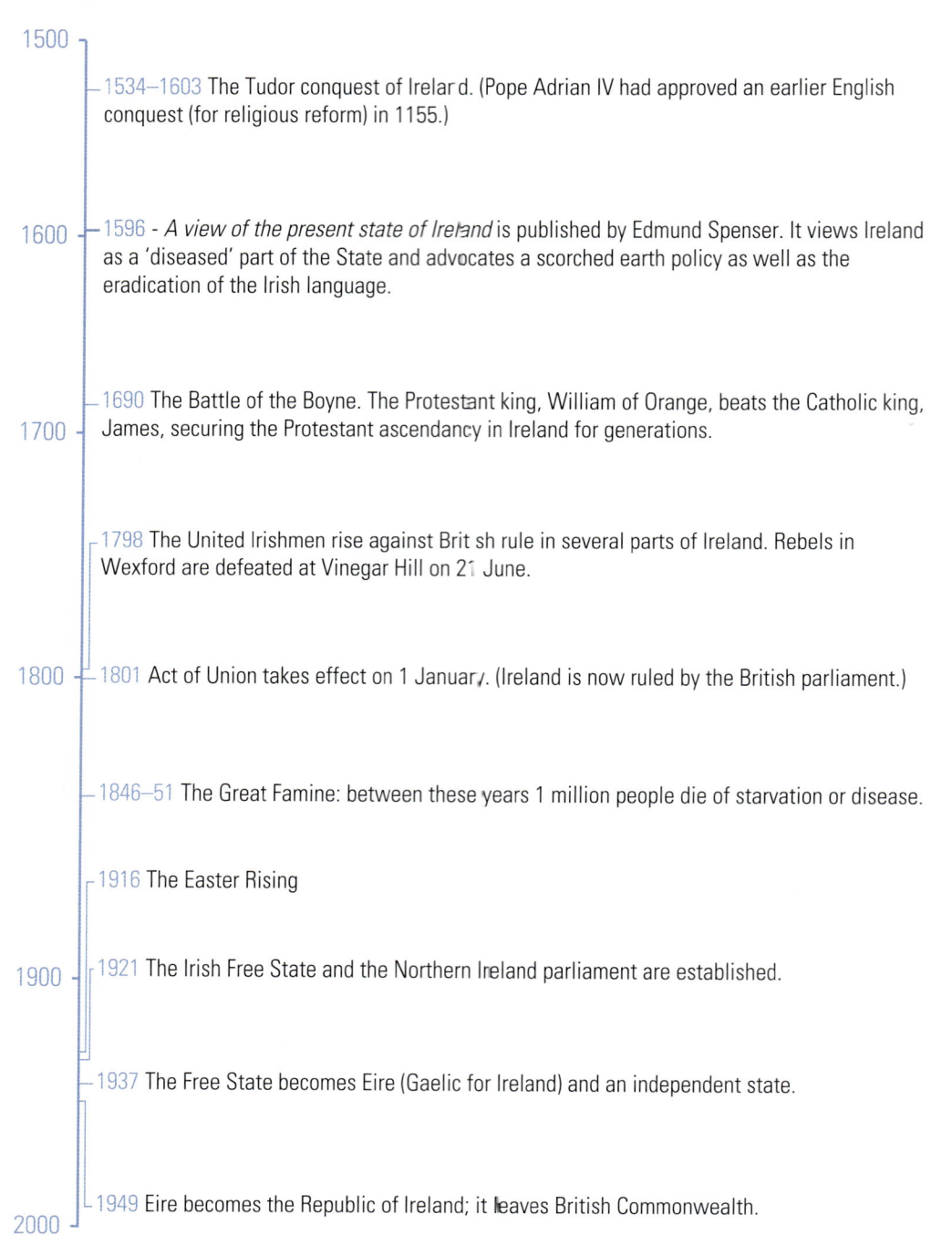

Timeline of events in Irish history 1534–1949

(These timelines are selective and focus on events that are mentioned, or alluded to, in *New Selected Poems*)

1534–1603 The Tudor conquest of Ireland. (Pope Adrian IV had approved an earlier English conquest (for religious reform) in 1155.)

1596 - *A view of the present state of Ireland* is published by Edmund Spenser. It views Ireland as a 'diseased' part of the State and advocates a scorched earth policy as well as the eradication of the Irish language.

1690 The Battle of the Boyne. The Protestant king, William of Orange, beats the Catholic king, James, securing the Protestant ascendancy in Ireland for generations.

1798 The United Irishmen rise against British rule in several parts of Ireland. Rebels in Wexford are defeated at Vinegar Hill on 21 June.

1801 Act of Union takes effect on 1 January. (Ireland is now ruled by the British parliament.)

1846–51 The Great Famine: between these years 1 million people die of starvation or disease.

1916 The Easter Rising

1921 The Irish Free State and the Northern Ireland parliament are established.

1937 The Free State becomes Eire (Gaelic for Ireland) and an independent state.

1949 Eire becomes the Republic of Ireland; it leaves British Commonwealth.

Timeline of events in Irish history 1966–1987

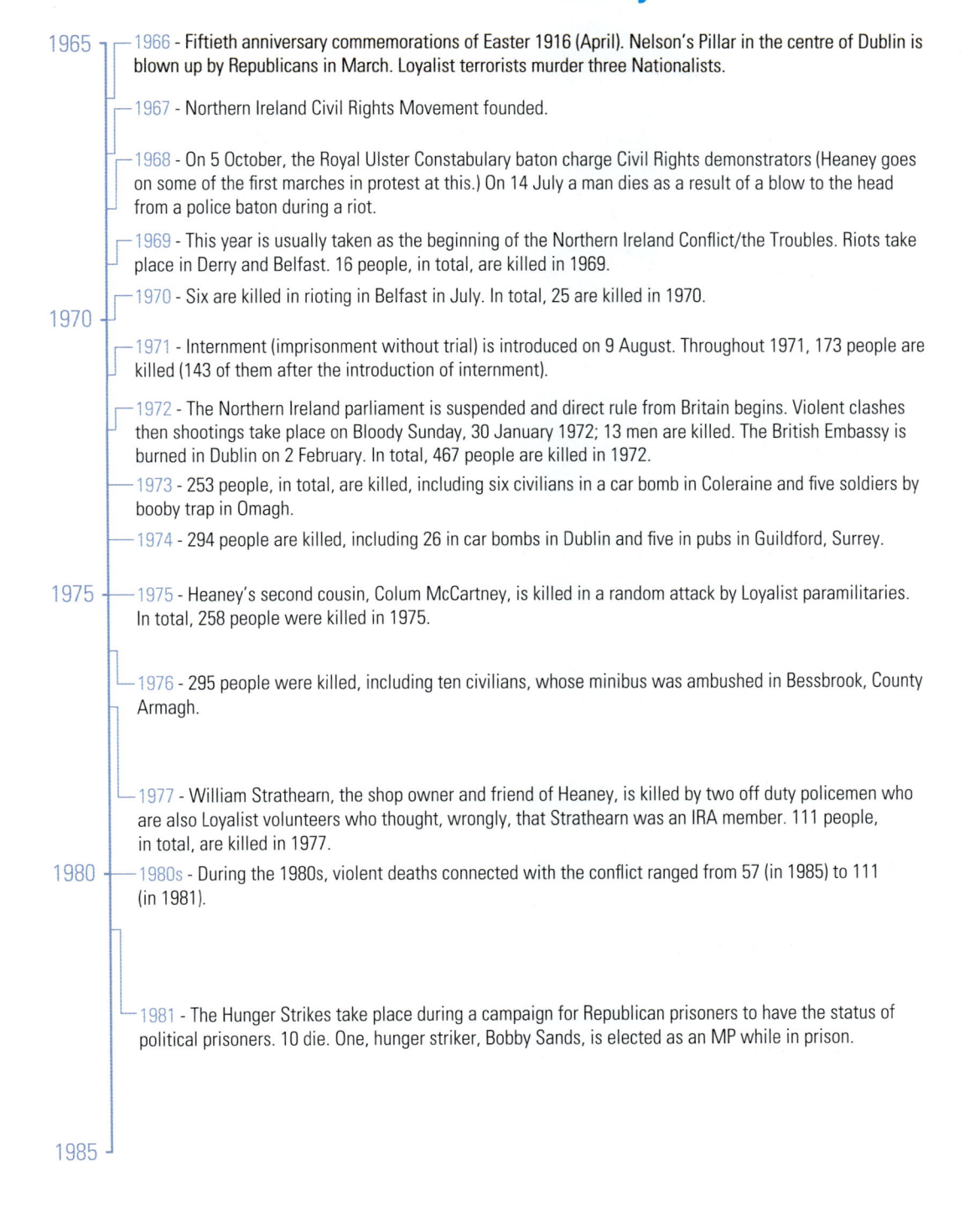

1965

1966 - Fiftieth anniversary commemorations of Easter 1916 (April). Nelson's Pillar in the centre of Dublin is blown up by Republicans in March. Loyalist terrorists murder three Nationalists.

1967 - Northern Ireland Civil Rights Movement founded.

1968 - On 5 October, the Royal Ulster Constabulary baton charge Civil Rights demonstrators (Heaney goes on some of the first marches in protest at this.) On 14 July a man dies as a result of a blow to the head from a police baton during a riot.

1969 - This year is usually taken as the beginning of the Northern Ireland Conflict/the Troubles. Riots take place in Derry and Belfast. 16 people, in total, are killed in 1969.

1970 - Six are killed in rioting in Belfast in July. In total, 25 are killed in 1970.

1970

1971 - Internment (imprisonment without trial) is introduced on 9 August. Throughout 1971, 173 people are killed (143 of them after the introduction of internment).

1972 - The Northern Ireland parliament is suspended and direct rule from Britain begins. Violent clashes then shootings take place on Bloody Sunday, 30 January 1972; 13 men are killed. The British Embassy is burned in Dublin on 2 February. In total, 467 people are killed in 1972.

1973 - 253 people, in total, are killed, including six civilians in a car bomb in Coleraine and five soldiers by booby trap in Omagh.

1974 - 294 people are killed, including 26 in car bombs in Dublin and five in pubs in Guildford, Surrey.

1975

1975 - Heaney's second cousin, Colum McCartney, is killed in a random attack by Loyalist paramilitaries. In total, 258 people were killed in 1975.

1976 - 295 people were killed, including ten civilians, whose minibus was ambushed in Bessbrook, County Armagh.

1977 - William Strathearn, the shop owner and friend of Heaney, is killed by two off duty policemen who are also Loyalist volunteers who thought, wrongly, that Strathearn was an IRA member. 111 people, in total, are killed in 1977.

1980

1980s - During the 1980s, violent deaths connected with the conflict ranged from 57 (in 1985) to 111 (in 1981).

1981 - The Hunger Strikes take place during a campaign for Republican prisoners to have the status of political prisoners. 10 die. One, hunger striker, Bobby Sands, is elected as an MP while in prison.

1985

NEW SELECTED POEMS 1966–1987

Map of Ireland

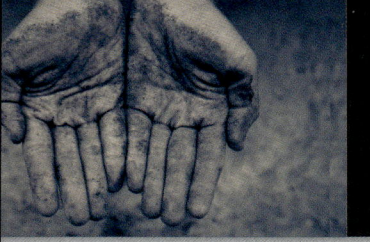

Taking it further

Prose by Heaney

Heaney, S. (1984) *Preoccupations: Selected Prose 1968–1978*, **Faber & Faber**

- Includes seminal essays such as 'From Monaghan to the Grand Canal' and 'The Sense of Place'

Heaney, S. (1988) *The Government of the Tongue*, **Faber & Faber**

- Offers insights on poetry and explores some of Heaney's international influences

Interviews

O'Driscoll, D. (2009) *Stepping Stones: Interviews with Seamus Heaney*, **Faber & Faber**

- Full of insight and interest, a superb book of far-reaching interviews

Criticism

Allen, M. (ed.) (1997) *Seamus Heaney (New Casebooks)*, **Macmillan**

- Essays by influential critics including Edna Longley, Christopher Ricks and Patricia Coughlan

Andrews, E. (1998) *The Poetry of Seamus Heaney*, **Columbia University Press**

- A survey of criticism, featuring extracts of significant essays, articles and books

Bloom, H. (ed.) (2003) *Seamus Heaney (Bloom's Major Poets)*, **Chelsea House**

- Considers some poems in depth, including 'The Harvest Bow' and 'The Haw Lantern'

Bloom, H. (ed.) (1986) *Seamus Heaney (Modern Critical Views)*, **Chelsea House**

- Critical essays on a range of topics in Heaney's work

Corcoran, N. (1998) *The Poetry of Seamus Heaney: A Critical Study*, **London: Faber & Faber**

- Detailed scholarly readings informed by historical approaches

Morrison, B. (1982) *Seamus Heaney (Contemporary Writers)*, **Methuen**

- An early study of the work up to and including *Field Work* that is perceptive and provocative by turns

O'Donoghue, B. (ed.) (2009), *The Cambridge Companion to Seamus Heaney,* **Cambridge University Press**

- Critical essays on topics ranging from the reception of Heaney's work to the ways in which his work explores femininity

Parker, M. (1993) *Seamus Heaney: The Making of the Poet,* **Gill and Macmillan**

- Thorough survey of Heaney's work up to and including *Seeing Things* (1991) that includes detailed close readings of many poems and makes good use of biographical contexts

Vendler, H. (2000) *Seamus Heaney,* **Harvard University Press**

- Insightful readings that trace Heaney's development as a poet and use a range of scholarly approaches

Selected websites

http://www.seamusheaneyhome.com

- The website of the Seamus Heaney HomePlace, which opened in Bellaghy, the village of Heaney's birth on 30 September 2016. Housed in a former police station, the £4 million centre includes a performance space and the exhibition includes some of Heaney's possessions and books as well as a recreation of his study.

http://www.bbc.co.uk/history/troubles

- A detailed and accessible website for the Northern Ireland Conflict.

http://www.nobelprize.org/nobel_prizes/literature/laureates/1995/heaney-facts.html

- Information and resources about Seamus Heaney from the official website of the Nobel prize.

STUDY AND REVISE for AS/A-level

Read, analyse and **revise** your set texts throughout the course to achieve your very best grade, with support at every stage from expert teachers and examiners.

Your year-round course companions for English literature

Each book contains:
- In-depth analysis of the text, from characterisation and themes to form, structure and language
- Thought-provoking tasks that develop your critical skills and personal response to the text
- Critical viewpoints to extend your understanding and prepare you for higher-level study

Titles in the series:
- A Room with a View
- A Streetcar Named Desire
- AQA A Poetry Anthology
- Atonement
- King Lear
- Measure for Measure
- Othello
- Seamus Heaney: Selected Poems
- Skirrid Hill
- Tess of the D'Urbervilles
- The Duchess of Malfi
- The Great Gatsby
- The Handmaid's Tale
- The Taming of the Shrew
- The Tempest
- The Wife of Bath's Tale
- The Winter's Tale
- Top Girls
- Wuthering Heights

£8.99 each

View the full series and order online at
www.hoddereducation.co.uk/studyandrevise

HODDER EDUCATION
LEARN MORE